AI In Cloud Computing

The Future of Intelligent Cloud Solutions

Table of Contents

AI in Cloud Computing

Abstract

Artificial Intelligence (AI) and Cloud Computing are two of the most transformative forces in modern technology, driving innovation, efficiency, and scalability across industries. **"AI in Cloud Computing: The Future of Intelligent Cloud Solutions"** is a comprehensive companion guide that explores the intersection of these two technologies, providing a deep understanding of their fundamentals, integration strategies, real-world applications, and future implications.

The book begins with an **in-depth exploration of AI and Cloud Computing**, breaking down their core principles, architectures, and service models (IaaS, PaaS, and SaaS). It examines how Cloud Computing provides the computational power, scalability, and storage required for AI workloads, while AI enhances cloud environments through **automation, intelligent decision-making, and security enhancements**. Readers will gain insights into how cloud-based AI solutions power innovations such as **predictive analytics, natural language processing, computer vision, and autonomous systems**.

Moving beyond the basics, the book delves into **how AI-driven cloud services are transforming industries**, enabling smarter and more efficient processes. It highlights **intelligent SaaS applications, AI-enhanced cloud security, cloud-based machine learning platforms, and AI-powered DevOps automation**. Case studies from various sectors—including **healthcare, finance, smart cities, cybersecurity, and e-commerce**—illustrate the profound impact of AI-integrated cloud systems.

Security and compliance challenges are also explored, as AI plays a crucial role in **identifying threats, automating security protocols, and ensuring compliance with industry regulations**. Readers will learn about **AI-driven identity and access management, self-healing infrastructures, and real-time anomaly detection** in cloud environments. The discussion extends to **AI governance, ethical considerations, bias mitigation, and regulatory frameworks** that shape the responsible deployment of AI in cloud computing.

Finally, the book looks toward the **future of AI in Cloud Computing**, discussing emerging trends such as **autonomous cloud platforms, federated learning, AI-powered edge computing, and the potential impact of quantum computing on AI workloads**. It presents a forward-thinking perspective on how businesses and IT professionals can **leverage AI and Cloud Computing together to drive digital transformation, cost efficiency, and competitive advantage.**

With a blend of theoretical concepts, practical applications, industry insights, and future projections, **this book is an essential guide for cloud architects, AI engineers, IT professionals, business leaders, and technology enthusiasts.** Whether you are just beginning your journey into AI and Cloud Computing or seeking advanced strategies to optimize your cloud infrastructure with AI, this guide provides **valuable knowledge, expert insights, and actionable recommendations** to help you navigate the evolving landscape of intelligent cloud solutions.

Part 1: Fundamentals of AI and Cloud Computing

Chapter 1: Introduction to AI and Cloud Computing

Introduction

Artificial Intelligence (AI) and Cloud Computing are two of the most transformative technologies of the digital era. AI enables machines to perform tasks that typically require human intelligence, such as learning, reasoning, and problem-solving. Meanwhile, Cloud Computing provides on-demand access to computing resources over the internet, enabling scalable and cost-efficient solutions. The convergence of AI and Cloud Computing has revolutionized industries, enabling businesses to harness the power of AI without the constraints of traditional IT infrastructure. This chapter explores the fundamental concepts of AI and Cloud Computing, their interdependence, and the benefits of integrating AI within the cloud ecosystem.

What is Artificial Intelligence?

Artificial Intelligence (AI) is a branch of computer science focused on developing machines that can perform tasks requiring human intelligence. AI systems leverage large datasets, advanced algorithms, and computational power to automate processes, enhance decision-making, and solve complex problems.

AI has revolutionized multiple industries by enabling intelligent automation, optimizing business operations, and facilitating data-driven insights. From self-driving cars to smart assistants, AI is shaping the future of technology.

Key Subfields of AI

1. Machine Learning (ML)

Machine Learning (ML) is a subset of AI that enables computers to learn patterns from data and improve performance without being explicitly programmed. ML models use statistical techniques to identify trends and make predictions. Common types of ML include:

- **Supervised Learning:** The model is trained on labeled data, learning to associate inputs with known outputs (e.g., email spam detection).
- **Unsupervised Learning:** The model identifies hidden patterns in unlabeled data (e.g., customer segmentation).
- **Reinforcement Learning:** The model learns through trial and error, optimizing actions based on rewards (e.g., game-playing AI like AlphaGo).

2. Deep Learning (DL)

Deep Learning is a specialized branch of ML that utilizes multi-layered neural networks to process complex data. Inspired by the human brain, deep learning models are particularly effective in:

- **Image and Speech Recognition:** Used in applications like facial recognition and voice assistants (e.g., Siri, Alexa).
- **Autonomous Vehicles:** Self-driving cars rely on deep learning for real-time decision-making.
- **Medical Diagnosis:** AI-powered systems detect diseases through medical imaging analysis.

3. Natural Language Processing (NLP)

Natural Language Processing (NLP) allows machines to understand, interpret, and generate human language. NLP enables applications such as:

- **Chatbots and Virtual Assistants:** AI-powered bots like ChatGPT and Google Assistant facilitate human-like conversations.
- **Language Translation:** NLP models power tools like Google Translate.
- **Sentiment Analysis:** Businesses analyze customer feedback to understand emotions and opinions.

4. Computer Vision

Computer Vision enables AI systems to interpret and analyze visual data from the real world. It is widely used in:

- **Facial Recognition:** Security systems authenticate users based on facial features.
- **Medical Imaging:** AI helps radiologists detect anomalies in X-rays and MRIs.
- **Retail and E-Commerce:** AI-powered image search improves shopping experiences.

5. Expert Systems

Expert Systems are AI applications designed to mimic human decision-making in specialized fields. They are used in:

- **Healthcare:** AI assists doctors in diagnosing diseases.
- **Finance:** AI evaluates creditworthiness and detects fraudulent transactions.

- **Legal Industry:** AI helps lawyers analyze case law and predict outcomes.

6. Reinforcement Learning (RL)

Reinforcement Learning involves training an AI agent through rewards and penalties. It is widely used in:

- **Gaming AI:** AI-driven players improve their strategies in complex games.
- **Robotics:** Autonomous robots learn to navigate dynamic environments.
- **Optimization Problems:** AI enhances supply chain logistics and resource allocation.

7. Explainable AI (XAI)

Explainable AI (XAI) focuses on making AI models interpretable and transparent, addressing concerns related to:

- **Bias and Fairness:** Ensuring AI decisions are ethical and unbiased.
- **Trust and Compliance:** Meeting regulatory requirements for AI applications in sensitive domains like healthcare and finance.

Applications of AI

AI is transforming numerous industries by providing intelligent solutions that drive efficiency and innovation:

1. Healthcare

- AI-powered diagnostic tools assist doctors in detecting diseases early.
- Personalized medicine tailors treatments based on genetic data.

- AI accelerates drug discovery, reducing research costs and time.

2. Finance

- AI-powered fraud detection identifies suspicious transactions.
- Algorithmic trading enables rapid, data-driven stock market investments.
- AI chatbots provide financial advisory services.

3. Retail and E-Commerce

- AI-powered recommendation engines personalize shopping experiences.
- Inventory management optimizes supply chain logistics.
- AI chatbots enhance customer support.

4. Cybersecurity

- AI detects and mitigates cyber threats in real-time.
- Automated security protocols strengthen enterprise networks.
- AI-driven analytics improve threat intelligence.

5. Autonomous Vehicles

- Self-driving cars rely on AI for object recognition and navigation.
- AI enhances driver assistance systems in modern vehicles.

6. Smart Assistants and IoT

- AI-powered smart assistants like Alexa and Google Assistant manage smart home devices.
- AI integrates with IoT (Internet of Things) to optimize energy consumption and security.

What is Cloud Computing?

Cloud Computing is a technology that enables businesses and individuals to access computing resources over the internet without relying on local infrastructure. Cloud providers offer scalable, on-demand services, reducing the need for costly hardware investments.

Key Characteristics of Cloud Computing

1. On-Demand Self-Service

Users can provision computing resources as needed without manual intervention.

2. Scalability and Elasticity

Cloud environments can dynamically scale up or down based on demand, optimizing performance and cost.

3. Pay-as-You-Go Pricing

Users pay only for the resources they consume, making cloud computing cost-effective.

4. Multi-Tenancy

Multiple users share cloud resources securely, optimizing resource utilization.

5. High Availability and Reliability

Cloud providers ensure redundancy, data backups, and disaster recovery mechanisms to prevent downtime.

Cloud Service Models

Traditional IT	Infrastructure (as a Service)	Platform (as a Service)	Software (as a Service)
Applications	Applications	Applications	Applications
Data	Data	Data	Data
Runtime	Runtime	Runtime	Runtime
Middleware	Middleware	Middleware	Middleware
Operating System	Operating System	Operating System	Operating System
Virtualization	Virtualization	Virtualization	Virtualization
Servers	Servers	Servers	Servers
Storage	Storage	Storage	Storage
Networking	Networking	Networking	Networking

1. Infrastructure as a Service (IaaS)

IaaS provides virtualized computing resources, such as:

- **Compute Power:** Virtual machines (e.g., AWS EC2, Azure Virtual Machines).
- **Storage:** Cloud storage solutions (e.g., Amazon S3, Google Cloud Storage).
- **Networking:** Virtual networks and firewalls (e.g., AWS VPC, Azure Virtual Network).

2. Platform as a Service (PaaS)

PaaS offers development platforms and tools for application deployment, including:

- **Cloud Databases:** Managed database services (e.g., Google Cloud SQL, AWS RDS).
- **Application Hosting:** Web app platforms (e.g., Azure App Services, Google App Engine).

- **Development Frameworks:** AI and ML tools (e.g., TensorFlow on Google Cloud).

3. Software as a Service (SaaS)

SaaS delivers cloud-hosted applications accessible via web browsers, such as:

- **Productivity Tools:** Google Workspace, Microsoft 365.
- **CRM Systems:** Salesforce, HubSpot.
- **Cloud Storage:** Dropbox, OneDrive.

Cloud Deployment Models

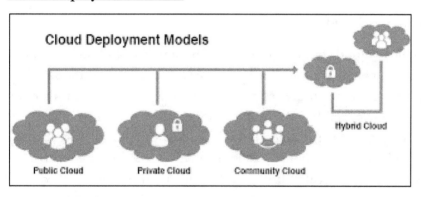

1. Public Cloud

A **public cloud** is a cloud computing model where services are hosted on a shared infrastructure and made available to multiple users over the internet. This model offers scalability, cost-effectiveness, and ease of access, making it ideal for startups, enterprises, and individual users. Public cloud providers own and manage the infrastructure, handling maintenance, security, and updates. Some of the most popular public cloud providers include **Amazon Web Services (AWS), Microsoft Azure, and Google Cloud Platform (GCP)**. While public clouds offer **high availability and global reach**, organizations must carefully manage data security and compliance requirements in shared environments.

2. Private Cloud

A **private cloud** is a cloud environment dedicated to a single organization, providing enhanced security, control, and customization. Unlike public clouds, private clouds are either hosted **on-premises or by a third-party provider** but remain exclusively used by one entity. This model is particularly beneficial for industries with **strict regulatory requirements**, such as healthcare, finance, and government institutions. Private clouds offer greater **data privacy, compliance, and performance optimization**, but they often come with **higher costs and maintenance responsibilities**. Organizations that prioritize **data sovereignty and high-security standards** often choose private cloud deployments.

3. Hybrid Cloud

A **hybrid cloud** combines elements of both **public and private clouds**, enabling organizations to **leverage the benefits of both models**. This approach allows businesses to keep sensitive workloads in a **private cloud** while utilizing the **public cloud** for less critical applications, ensuring a balance between **flexibility, cost efficiency, and security**. Hybrid cloud solutions enable seamless data migration, **disaster recovery**, and **scalability**, making them an excellent choice for organizations with dynamic computing needs. Many enterprises adopt hybrid clouds to **optimize resource utilization, ensure business continuity, and maintain compliance** while still taking advantage of the public cloud's affordability and scalability.

4. Multi-Cloud

A **multi-cloud** strategy involves using multiple **cloud providers** to enhance performance, **reduce dependency on a single vendor**, and improve compliance with global regulations. By distributing workloads across different cloud environments, organizations can optimize cost, avoid vendor lock-in, and **improve redundancy and fault tolerance**. Multi-cloud deployments are increasingly popular in industries that **require high availability, regional compliance, and customized**

cloud services. However, managing multiple cloud platforms requires **robust orchestration, security policies, and integration tools** to ensure smooth operations and minimize complexity.

5. Community Cloud

A community cloud is a cloud computing model where the infrastructure is shared among multiple organizations with common concerns, such as security, compliance, or industry-specific requirements. This model is often used by industries like healthcare, finance, education, and government, where organizations need to adhere to similar regulatory standards while benefiting from shared cloud resources. Community clouds provide a balance between cost-effectiveness and security, offering greater control than public clouds while maintaining a collaborative and cost-sharing approach. However, governance and management of shared resources must be clearly defined to ensure efficient operation and security compliance.

Benefits of Cloud Computing

1. Cost Efficiency: Reduces infrastructure costs by eliminating expensive hardware investments.

2. Flexibility and Scalability: Allows businesses to scale IT resources up or down based on demand.

3. Security and Compliance: Leading cloud providers implement stringent security measures, including encryption and identity management.

4. Business Continuity: Disaster recovery solutions ensure high availability and minimal downtime.

5. Remote Work and Collaboration: Cloud services enable remote access to applications, improving team collaboration.

The Convergence of AI and Cloud Computing

The integration of **Artificial Intelligence (AI) and Cloud Computing** has led to transformative advancements across industries. Cloud platforms provide an ideal foundation for developing, training, and deploying AI-driven solutions at scale. This convergence enhances **innovation, operational efficiency, and accessibility**, making AI-driven insights more attainable for businesses of all sizes.

Cloud-based AI enables organizations to **process massive datasets, execute complex algorithms, and deploy intelligent applications without requiring extensive on-premises infrastructure**. This has led to smarter applications, enhanced automation, and improved decision-making across multiple domains.

Key Advantages of AI-Driven Cloud Computing

1. Scalability: Unleashing AI's Full Potential

AI applications often require extensive computational resources, especially for **machine learning (ML) model training, deep learning, and large-scale data processing**. Cloud computing provides **on-demand, elastic resources** that allow organizations to:

- Scale AI workloads dynamically based on demand.
- Train deep learning models on high-performance GPUs and TPUs.
- Deploy AI models across global data centers without hardware constraints.

Cloud providers such as **AWS, Microsoft Azure, and Google Cloud** offer **autoscaling capabilities**, ensuring that AI applications can scale seamlessly during peak workloads.

2. Data Storage and High-Speed Processing

AI models thrive on vast amounts of data, and cloud platforms provide **cost-effective, high-performance storage and processing power**. Benefits include:

- **Data Lakes and Warehouses:** Cloud-based storage solutions (e.g., Amazon S3, Google BigQuery, Azure Data Lake) efficiently handle structured and unstructured data.
- **High-Speed Processing:** AI algorithms leverage cloud-based GPUs and TPUs to accelerate training and inference.
- **Edge AI Integration:** AI models can process real-time data at the edge, reducing latency and improving responsiveness.

With cloud-based AI, businesses can process **terabytes or even petabytes of data** in real-time, enhancing insights and automation.

3. Prebuilt AI Services and APIs

Major cloud providers offer **prebuilt AI and ML services** that simplify AI adoption without requiring extensive expertise in data science. These services include:

AI-Powered Cloud Services

- **Amazon SageMaker (AWS):** Enables ML model development, training, and deployment.
- **Azure AI (Microsoft):** Includes prebuilt AI services for vision, speech, and text analysis.
- **Google AI Platform:** Provides cloud-based tools for ML and deep learning development.

Cloud-Based AI APIs

- **Vision APIs:** Image recognition, object detection, and facial analysis. (e.g., Google Cloud Vision API, Amazon Rekognition)
- **Speech and Text APIs:** Voice recognition, language translation, and NLP. (e.g., Azure Speech Services, Google Cloud Natural Language API)
- **Chatbots and Conversational AI:** Virtual assistants powered by AI-driven cloud services. (e.g., AWS Lex, Google Dialogflow)

These prebuilt AI services allow businesses to **integrate AI capabilities quickly and efficiently**, reducing development costs and time-to-market.

4. Cost Efficiency: AI Without Heavy Hardware Investments

Traditional AI infrastructure requires **expensive hardware, data centers, and ongoing maintenance**. Cloud computing eliminates these constraints, offering:

- **Pay-as-You-Go Pricing:** Businesses only pay for the computing power and storage they use.
- **No Upfront Infrastructure Costs:** AI models can be trained and deployed without on-premises hardware.
- **Optimized Resource Allocation:** Serverless computing (e.g., AWS Lambda, Azure Functions) ensures AI workloads run efficiently.

This cost-effective approach makes **AI adoption more accessible for startups, enterprises, and researchers.**

Real-World Applications of AI-Powered Cloud Solutions

1. Automated Customer Support and Chatbots

AI-driven **virtual assistants and chatbots** hosted on the cloud provide:

- 24/7 customer support with real-time responses.
- Sentiment analysis to understand customer emotions.
- Multilingual support through NLP-powered translation services.

Examples:

- **Google Dialogflow** powers intelligent virtual agents for businesses.
- **AWS Lex** enables voice and text-based conversational AI.
- **Azure Bot Services** integrates AI-driven chatbots into enterprise applications.

2. Predictive Analytics for Business Intelligence

Cloud-based AI enables organizations to **analyze historical data and predict future trends**. Applications include:

- **Retail:** AI-driven demand forecasting for inventory management.
- **Healthcare:** Predictive analytics for early disease detection.
- **Finance:** AI-based fraud detection and risk assessment.

3. AI-Powered Cybersecurity Solutions

AI-driven **cloud security solutions** help detect and mitigate threats in real-time. Key capabilities include:

- **Threat Detection:** AI identifies anomalies in network traffic.
- **Automated Incident Response:** AI-powered security systems mitigate cyber threats autonomously.
- **Fraud Prevention:** Cloud-based AI detects suspicious transactions and unauthorized access.

Examples:

- **Microsoft Defender for Cloud**: AI-driven security management and threat protection.
- **Google Chronicle**: Cloud-native security analytics powered by AI.
- **AWS GuardDuty**: AI-based threat detection for AWS environments.

4. Autonomous Systems and IoT Integration

Cloud computing enables AI to power **autonomous devices and IoT ecosystems,** including:

- **Smart Cities:** AI optimizes traffic management, energy consumption, and public safety.
- **Self-Driving Vehicles:** Cloud-based AI processes real-time sensor data for autonomous navigation.
- **Industrial Automation:** AI-driven robots and IoT devices optimize manufacturing operations.

5. Healthcare Innovations with AI and Cloud

Cloud-hosted AI models are **transforming the healthcare industry** by:

- **Assisting in medical diagnosis** (e.g., AI analyzing X-rays and MRIs).
- **Enabling personalized medicine** by analyzing genetic data.
- **Improving patient monitoring** through AI-powered IoT devices.

Examples:

- **Google DeepMind Health**: AI-driven disease detection and patient care.
- **IBM Watson Health**: AI-powered insights for medical research.
- **AWS Comprehend Medical**: NLP-based medical data analysis.

Challenges and Future Trends in AI-Cloud Convergence

1. Data Privacy and Security

As AI models rely on **cloud-stored data**, organizations must address:

- **Data encryption and access control** to prevent breaches.
- **Regulatory compliance** (e.g., GDPR, HIPAA) for AI-driven applications.

2. Ethical AI and Bias Mitigation

- AI models must be designed to **avoid biases in decision-making**.
- Cloud providers are investing in **explainable AI (XAI)** for transparency.

3. Edge AI: The Next Frontier

- **Edge computing** brings AI closer to the data source, reducing latency.
- AI-powered **IoT devices and smart sensors** will enable real-time decision-making.

4. AI Democratization and No-Code AI

- Cloud providers are introducing **low-code/no-code AI platforms**, making AI accessible to non-technical users.
- **AI-as-a-Service (AIaaS)** will continue to grow, simplifying AI deployment.

Why AI Needs Cloud Computing and Vice Versa

Why AI Needs Cloud Computing:

1. **Computational Power**: AI models, particularly deep learning networks, require extensive computational resources that cloud providers efficiently deliver.

2. **Big Data Management**: Cloud storage enables AI to access and process large datasets for training and analysis.

3. **Collaboration and Accessibility**: Cloud-based AI platforms facilitate remote access and collaborative development among data scientists and engineers.

4. **Rapid Experimentation and Deployment**: AI models can be trained, tested, and deployed faster in cloud environments.

Why Cloud Computing Needs AI:

1. **Automated Management**: AI enhances cloud operations through predictive maintenance, resource optimization, and automated scaling.

2. **Security and Threat Detection**: AI-powered analytics in the cloud improves cybersecurity by identifying anomalies and preventing data breaches.

3. **Enhanced Data Analytics**: AI helps organizations extract meaningful insights from cloud-stored data, driving data-driven decision-making.

4. **Optimized Cloud Services**: AI automates routine cloud tasks, reducing manual efforts and improving efficiency.

The interdependence of AI and Cloud Computing is shaping the future of IT, enabling intelligent automation, smarter applications, and seamless digital transformation.

Key Benefits of AI in the Cloud

1. Cost Savings

Cloud-based AI eliminates the need for expensive on-premises infrastructure, reducing capital expenditure while offering pay-as-you-go models.

2. Scalability

Organizations can scale AI workloads up or down based on demand, making cloud computing ideal for dynamic and resource-intensive AI applications.

3. Faster AI Model Training and Deployment

Cloud platforms provide optimized AI services that accelerate model training, validation, and deployment, reducing time-to-market.

4. Access to Advanced AI Tools

Cloud providers offer AI and machine learning services, such as AWS SageMaker, Google AI, and Azure Machine Learning, enabling businesses to integrate AI without deep technical expertise.

5. Improved Security and Compliance

Cloud AI services include built-in security features like encryption, threat detection, and compliance with industry regulations, ensuring data privacy and protection.

6. Democratization of AI

Cloud-based AI services make AI accessible to businesses of all sizes, enabling startups and enterprises to leverage AI without extensive infrastructure investments.

Summary

The fusion of AI and Cloud Computing is reshaping the digital landscape, driving automation, intelligence, and efficiency across industries. AI enables machines to learn, analyze, and make decisions, while Cloud Computing provides the necessary infrastructure for AI development and deployment. Their convergence offers unparalleled scalability, cost savings, and access to powerful AI-driven applications. As businesses increasingly adopt AI in the cloud, they unlock new opportunities for innovation, enhanced decision-making, and smarter digital transformation. The following chapters will explore deeper technical aspects, real-world applications, and strategies for leveraging AI in cloud environments effectively.

Chapter 2: Core Concepts of Artificial Intelligence

Introduction

Artificial Intelligence (AI) has rapidly transformed industries by enabling machines to perform cognitive tasks traditionally associated with human intelligence. At its core, AI encompasses a wide range of techniques, including Machine Learning (ML), Deep Learning (DL), Neural Networks, Natural Language Processing (NLP), and Computer Vision. This chapter delves into these fundamental concepts and explores how AI algorithms function within cloud-based AI solutions. Additionally, we examine the critical role of Large Language Models (LLMs) in the evolution of AI-driven applications.

Machine Learning (ML), Deep Learning (DL), and Neural Networks

Artificial Intelligence (AI) is revolutionizing industries by enabling machines to learn from data, make decisions, and perform complex tasks. Among its core technologies, **Machine Learning (ML), Deep Learning (DL), and Neural Networks** form the backbone of intelligent systems. These technologies power everything from recommendation engines and fraud detection to autonomous vehicles and medical diagnostics.

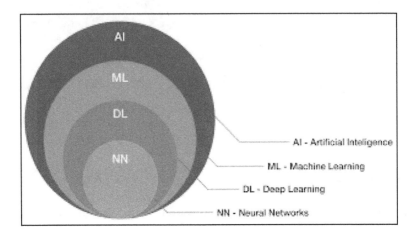

Machine Learning (ML)

What is Machine Learning?

Machine Learning (ML) is a subset of AI that enables systems to **learn from data and improve their performance over time without explicit programming**. ML algorithms analyze data, identify patterns, and make predictions or decisions based on those patterns. This ability to **automate learning from experience** is what makes ML a powerful tool in various applications, from financial forecasting to healthcare diagnostics.

Types of Machine Learning

ML can be broadly classified into three major types:

1. Supervised Learning

- The model is trained on **labeled data**, where each input is associated with a known output.
- It **learns a mapping function** from input to output, enabling it to make accurate predictions on new, unseen data.
- **Examples:**

- o **Spam Detection:** Identifying emails as spam or non-spam based on past labeled examples.
- o **Fraud Prevention:** Detecting fraudulent transactions by analyzing historical patterns.
- o **Medical Diagnosis:** Predicting diseases from patient data using labeled medical records.

2. Unsupervised Learning

- The model learns **without labeled data**, identifying underlying structures and relationships in the dataset.
- It is often used for **clustering, anomaly detection, and association rule learning**.
- **Examples:**
  - o **Customer Segmentation:** Grouping customers based on purchasing behavior.
  - o **Anomaly Detection:** Identifying unusual transactions in financial systems.
  - o **Market Basket Analysis:** Discovering product relationships for better recommendations.

3. Reinforcement Learning

- The model learns by **interacting with an environment** and receiving feedback in the form of **rewards or penalties**.
- It is widely used in **robotics, gaming, and autonomous systems**.
- **Examples:**
  - o **Autonomous Vehicles:** Learning to navigate by optimizing routes.
  - o **Game-Playing AI:** AI like AlphaGo mastering board games through self-play.
  - o **Industrial Automation:** Optimizing manufacturing processes to improve efficiency.

Deep Learning (DL)

What is Deep Learning?

Deep Learning (DL) is an advanced branch of ML that leverages **deep neural networks** to model complex relationships in data. Unlike traditional ML, DL can process **large-scale unstructured data**, such as images, speech, and text, making it the driving force behind **AI advancements in computer vision, natural language processing (NLP), and autonomous systems**.

Key Deep Learning Architectures

Deep learning models vary based on the task they are designed to perform. Some of the most commonly used architectures include:

1. Convolutional Neural Networks (CNNs): Powering Image Recognition

- CNNs specialize in **image processing** by detecting patterns like edges, textures, and shapes.
- They use **convolutional layers** to extract features and **pooling layers** to reduce dimensionality.
- **Applications:**
    - **Facial Recognition:** Unlocking smartphones using facial features.
    - **Medical Imaging:** Detecting diseases in X-rays and MRIs.
    - **Autonomous Vehicles:** Identifying road signs and pedestrians.

2. Recurrent Neural Networks (RNNs): Understanding Sequential Data

- RNNs are designed for **processing sequences**, such as time-series data, speech, and text.

- They use **feedback loops** to retain memory from previous inputs, making them ideal for tasks that require context awareness.
- **Applications:**
    - **Speech Recognition:** Transcribing spoken words into text (e.g., Siri, Google Assistant).
    - **Time-Series Forecasting:** Predicting stock prices based on historical trends.
    - **Chatbots:** Understanding and responding to human conversations.

3. Transformers: Revolutionizing Natural Language Processing (NLP)

- Transformers, such as **GPT (Generative Pre-trained Transformer) and BERT (Bidirectional Encoder Representations from Transformers)**, are the most advanced architectures for **text understanding and generation.**
- They use **self-attention mechanisms** to process words in context rather than in isolation.
- **Applications:**
    - **Chatbots and Virtual Assistants:** Powering AI-driven assistants like ChatGPT and Alexa.
    - **Machine Translation:** Translating text between languages (e.g., Google Translate).
    - **Text Generation:** Writing coherent articles, reports, and code snippets.

Neural Networks: The Building Blocks of AI

What are Neural Networks?

Neural Networks are the **core technology behind deep learning**. Inspired by the human brain, they consist of **layers of interconnected**

neurons that process and transform data. These networks can learn **complex relationships** and make highly accurate predictions.

Structure of Neural Networks

A neural network consists of three main layers:

1. Input Layer: Receiving Raw Data

- This layer **takes in raw data** such as images, text, or numerical values.
- The input data is **converted into numerical representations** that the network can process.
- **Example:** In an image recognition task, pixel values from an image are fed into the network.

2. Hidden Layers: Extracting Features and Patterns

- These layers perform **complex computations**, detecting important features in data.
- Each neuron applies **weights and activation functions** to transform input data.
- Deep networks with multiple hidden layers can **learn hierarchical patterns**.
- **Example:** A CNN's hidden layers might first detect edges, then textures, then entire objects in an image.

3. Output Layer: Making Predictions

- The final layer produces the **network's decision or prediction**.
- It applies **activation functions** like softmax or sigmoid to generate output values.
- **Example:** A sentiment analysis model outputs "positive" or "negative" sentiment based on text input.

Types of Neural Networks

Neural networks can be adapted for various tasks, including:

- **Feedforward Neural Networks (FNNs):** Basic neural networks where data flows in one direction (used in simple classification tasks).
- **Convolutional Neural Networks (CNNs):** Specialized for image and video analysis.
- **Recurrent Neural Networks (RNNs):** Designed for sequential data like speech and time series.
- **Generative Adversarial Networks (GANs):** Used for generating realistic images, videos, and even synthetic human voices.

AI Algorithms and Their Role in Cloud-Based AI Solutions

Artificial Intelligence (AI) algorithms are the core components that drive intelligent decision-making, automation, and predictive analytics. These algorithms process vast amounts of data, recognize patterns, and generate meaningful insights that enhance various applications across industries. AI algorithms are categorized based on their functions, learning approaches, and complexity levels.

Common AI Algorithms and Their Applications

AI algorithms can be broadly classified into traditional machine learning techniques and advanced deep learning models. Below are some widely used AI algorithms:

1. Decision Trees

Decision trees are hierarchical models used for both classification and regression tasks. They split data into branches based on specific conditions, making them highly interpretable and easy to understand. Decision trees are commonly applied in medical diagnosis, customer segmentation, and financial risk assessment.

2. Support Vector Machines (SVMs)

SVMs are powerful classification algorithms that work by finding an optimal hyperplane to separate data points in a high-dimensional space. They are particularly effective for text classification, handwriting recognition, and image categorization.

3. K-Nearest Neighbors (KNN)

KNN is a simple yet effective instance-based learning algorithm that classifies new data points based on their similarity to existing labeled examples. It is widely used in recommendation systems, pattern recognition, and anomaly detection.

4. Gradient Boosting Machines (GBMs)

Gradient Boosting Machines (GBMs) are ensemble learning techniques that combine multiple weak models to create a strong predictive model. Popular GBM implementations include **XGBoost**, **LightGBM**, and **CatBoost**. These algorithms are widely used in predictive modeling tasks such as sales forecasting, fraud detection, and risk management.

5. Neural Networks

Neural networks form the foundation of deep learning and are designed to mimic the structure of the human brain. These networks excel in recognizing patterns in complex and unstructured data, such as images, speech, and text. Neural networks are extensively used in **natural language processing (NLP), autonomous driving, image classification, and speech recognition.**

Cloud-Based AI Solutions and Their Advantages

Cloud platforms provide a scalable and efficient environment for training and deploying AI models. Organizations are increasingly adopting cloud-based AI solutions to harness the power of machine learning and deep learning without the need for extensive on-premises infrastructure.

1. Scalability and Performance

Cloud platforms, such as AWS, Microsoft Azure, and Google Cloud, offer high-performance computing resources that allow AI models to be trained and deployed at scale. Businesses can process large datasets and perform computations efficiently, reducing time-to-market for AI-driven applications.

2. Cost-Effectiveness

Cloud-based AI solutions eliminate the need for expensive hardware and maintenance costs. Companies can leverage **pay-as-you-go pricing models** to optimize costs and scale resources as needed, making AI adoption more accessible.

3. Real-Time Data Processing

AI-powered cloud solutions enable real-time data processing, which is crucial for industries such as finance, healthcare, and cybersecurity. Examples include:

- **Predictive analytics in business intelligence:** AI algorithms analyze historical data to forecast trends and drive data-driven decision-making.
- **Fraud detection in financial services:** Machine learning models identify suspicious transactions and prevent fraudulent activities in real-time.

- **Automated diagnostics in healthcare:** AI-powered cloud platforms assist medical professionals by analyzing medical images, detecting anomalies, and providing early disease diagnosis.

4. Integration with Advanced AI Services

Leading cloud providers offer AI services such as **Google Cloud AI, AWS AI & Machine Learning Services, and Microsoft Azure AI**. These platforms provide pre-trained models, APIs, and automated machine learning (AutoML) tools that accelerate AI adoption across industries.

The Role of Large Language Models (LLMs) in AI

Large Language Models (LLMs) represent a transformative leap in artificial intelligence, enabling machines to understand, generate, and interact with human language at an unprecedented level. These models, such as **OpenAI's GPT, Google's Gemini, and Meta's LLaMA**, leverage **deep learning architectures and vast datasets** to produce context-aware responses across a wide range of applications. By processing massive amounts of text, LLMs have become essential in **natural language processing (NLP), automated content generation, and intelligent decision-making.**

How Large Language Models Enhance AI Autonomy

The increasing sophistication of LLMs has contributed to greater AI autonomy, allowing machines to perform complex tasks without direct human intervention. Key capabilities that enhance AI autonomy include:

1. Contextual Understanding

LLMs can process and retain context over long conversations, making them ideal for applications such as chatbots, virtual assistants, and customer support systems. By understanding previous interactions, they deliver **coherent, relevant, and contextually aware responses** rather than isolated or generic answers.

2. Zero-Shot and Few-Shot Learning

Unlike traditional AI models that require extensive training on specific tasks, LLMs demonstrate **zero-shot** and **few-shot learning** capabilities.

- **Zero-shot learning** allows LLMs to handle new tasks without prior examples, leveraging their vast knowledge base to infer patterns.
- **Few-shot learning** enables them to quickly adapt to new tasks with minimal labeled examples, reducing the need for extensive retraining.

3. Multi-Task Learning

LLMs excel in performing multiple AI tasks simultaneously, making them highly versatile. Some common tasks include:

- **Language translation** across different dialects and linguistic structures
- **Summarization** of lengthy documents, legal papers, and research articles
- **Text generation** for creative writing, business reports, and marketing content

These abilities make LLMs a cornerstone for automating processes across industries, from **journalism and legal services to healthcare and finance**.

The Fusion of LLMs with Multi-Agent Architectures

A growing trend in AI is the integration of LLMs with **multi-agent architectures**, where multiple AI agents collaborate to complete tasks more efficiently. These agents specialize in different functions and work together to enhance AI-driven automation.

1. AI-Powered Chatbots in Customer Service

LLMs are widely deployed in customer service, **automating responses, handling inquiries, and even resolving complaints**. By integrating with multi-agent systems, chatbots can escalate complex queries to specialized AI agents, ensuring **faster resolution and enhanced user experience**.

2. Automated Report Generation and Data Summarization

Organizations leverage LLMs to **analyze vast amounts of data, extract key insights, and generate detailed reports**. AI agents can work together to **collect, process, and summarize** financial reports, market analysis, and research findings with **minimal human intervention**.

3. Intelligent Personal Assistants for Task Automation

LLMs power next-generation personal assistants that **manage schedules, draft emails, provide recommendations, and perform research**. By combining multiple AI agents—such as **speech recognition, contextual understanding, and decision-making modules**—these assistants can **streamline workflows and enhance productivity** for professionals.

Summary

This chapter explored the foundational concepts of AI, including Machine Learning, Deep Learning, and Neural Networks. It examined how NLP and Computer Vision enable AI to process human language and visual data. AI algorithms, from decision trees to neural networks, play a crucial role in cloud-based AI solutions. Additionally, Large Language Models (LLMs) have revolutionized AI's capabilities, enhancing automation, contextual understanding, and decision-making. As AI and cloud computing converge, these core concepts will drive the next wave of intelligent solutions across industries.

Chapter 3: Fundamentals of Cloud Computing

Introduction

Cloud computing has revolutionized the way businesses and individuals access, store, and process data. By providing on-demand computing resources over the internet, cloud computing enables organizations to scale their infrastructure dynamically and leverage advanced technologies without significant capital investment. This chapter explores the core fundamentals of cloud computing, including its models, environments, key service providers, and essential components such as storage, virtualization, and scalability.

Cloud Computing Models: IaaS, PaaS, SaaS

Cloud computing has revolutionized how businesses deploy, manage, and scale their IT resources. It offers **on-demand access to computing power, storage, and applications** without requiring extensive on-premises infrastructure. Cloud services are broadly categorized into **three primary models: Infrastructure as a Service (IaaS), Platform as a Service (PaaS), and Software as a Service (SaaS)**. Each model provides a different level of control, flexibility, and management, catering to specific business needs.

1. Infrastructure as a Service (IaaS)

Infrastructure as a Service (IaaS) provides organizations with **virtualized computing resources over the internet**, including servers, storage, networking, and virtualization. It eliminates the need for businesses to invest in **physical hardware**, allowing them to **scale resources on demand and pay only for what they use.**

Key Features

- **Scalability:** Organizations can increase or decrease computing power as needed.
- **Cost-Efficiency:** No upfront investment in hardware; costs are based on usage.
- **Flexibility:** Users have full control over their infrastructure, choosing their preferred **operating system, middleware, and applications.**

Common Use Cases

IaaS is widely used for:

- **Web Hosting:** Hosting websites and applications without maintaining physical servers.
- **Disaster Recovery:** Ensuring business continuity by backing up data in the cloud.
- **Big Data Analytics:** Running complex data processing tasks that require high computational power.

Examples of IaaS Providers

- **Amazon EC2 (Elastic Compute Cloud)** – Provides scalable virtual servers.
- **Microsoft Azure Virtual Machines** – Offers Windows and Linux-based virtual environments.
- **Google Compute Engine** – Delivers high-performance virtual machines with custom configurations.

2. Platform as a Service (PaaS)

Platform as a Service (PaaS) provides **a comprehensive cloud environment for application development, testing, and deployment.** It includes **operating systems, development frameworks, databases, and automation tools**, allowing developers to focus on coding rather than managing infrastructure.

Key Features

- **Rapid Development:** Pre-configured development tools speed up the application lifecycle.
- **Automatic Scaling:** Cloud providers handle resource allocation based on demand.
- **Integrated Development Environment (IDE):** Provides built-in support for multiple programming languages.

Common Use Cases

PaaS is widely used for:

- **Application Development:** Enabling developers to build, test, and deploy applications efficiently.
- **Microservices and API Management:** Supporting containerized applications and seamless API integration.
- **Enterprise Applications:** Powering internal business applications without requiring infrastructure management.

Examples of PaaS Providers

- **Google App Engine** – A fully managed platform for web and mobile applications.
- **Microsoft Azure App Service** – Provides hosting and development tools for web apps.

- **AWS Elastic Beanstalk** – Automatically manages deployment, scaling, and monitoring for applications.

3. Software as a Service (SaaS)

Software as a Service (SaaS) delivers **fully functional software applications over the internet**, eliminating the need for installation, maintenance, or updates on local devices. SaaS applications are accessible via a **web browser**, making them ideal for businesses that need scalable, **subscription-based software**.

Key Features

- **Accessibility:** Users can access SaaS applications from any device with an internet connection.
- **Automatic Updates:** Software updates and security patches are handled by the provider.
- **Multi-Tenancy:** A single application serves multiple customers with customizable settings.

Common Use Cases

SaaS is widely used for:

- **Collaboration and Communication:** Tools like Google Workspace and Microsoft Teams enable remote teamwork.
- **Customer Relationship Management (CRM):** Platforms like Salesforce streamline sales and marketing.
- **Email and Productivity Applications:** Microsoft Office 365 provides cloud-based document editing and collaboration.

Examples of SaaS Providers

- **Google Workspace (Gmail, Docs, Drive, Meet)** – Offers cloud-based productivity and collaboration tools.

- **Microsoft Office 365** – Provides access to Word, Excel, PowerPoint, and Outlook online.
- **Salesforce** – A leading CRM platform that automates sales and customer engagement.

Choosing the Right Cloud Model

Selecting the right cloud computing model depends on **business needs, technical expertise, and cost considerations**:

- **IaaS** is ideal for organizations needing **complete control over their infrastructure** while avoiding physical hardware investments.
- **PaaS** is best for **developers** who want to focus on **building and deploying applications** without managing servers.
- **SaaS** is suitable for **end-users** who require **ready-to-use software solutions** with minimal maintenance.

By leveraging the appropriate cloud computing model, businesses can **enhance scalability, improve efficiency, and reduce IT overhead costs**, making cloud adoption an essential strategy in today's digital landscape.

Public, Private, Hybrid, and Multi-Cloud Environments

Cloud computing offers businesses flexible and scalable solutions tailored to different operational and security needs. Depending on factors such as **cost, security, compliance, and performance**, organizations can choose from various cloud deployment models. The four primary types of cloud environments—**Public Cloud, Private Cloud, Hybrid Cloud, and Multi-Cloud**—each come with unique benefits and challenges, making it crucial to select the right model for specific business objectives.

1. Public Cloud

A **public cloud** is a cloud computing model where third-party providers offer **on-demand computing resources and services over the internet**. These providers manage infrastructure, maintenance, and security, allowing organizations to focus on their core business operations without investing in physical hardware. Public cloud services are typically offered through a **pay-as-you-go pricing model**, making them cost-effective for startups, enterprises, and individual users alike.

Key Features

- **Scalability:** Easily scale resources up or down based on demand.
- **Cost-Effectiveness:** No need to invest in on-premises infrastructure.
- **Accessibility:** Services are accessible from anywhere with an internet connection.

Pros

✓ **Lower Costs:** No capital expenditure; payment is based on usage.

✓ **Managed Services:** Providers handle maintenance, updates, and security.

✓ **Elasticity:** Ideal for dynamic workloads and rapid scaling.

Cons

✗ **Limited Control:** Businesses rely on third-party providers for security and infrastructure management.

✗ **Compliance Risks:** May not meet strict regulatory requirements for sensitive data.

Examples of Public Cloud Providers

- **Amazon Web Services (AWS)** – Offers a vast range of cloud services, from storage to AI capabilities.
- **Microsoft Azure** – Provides cloud computing solutions tailored for enterprises and developers.
- **Google Cloud Platform (GCP)** – Specializes in AI, machine learning, and scalable cloud solutions.

2. Private Cloud

A **private cloud** is a cloud computing environment **exclusively dedicated to a single organization**. It can be hosted on-premises or by a third-party provider but is **not shared with other users**. Private clouds provide businesses with **greater control over security, compliance, and customization**, making them ideal for industries handling sensitive data, such as **finance, healthcare, and government agencies**.

Key Features

- **Enhanced Security:** Resources are isolated from other organizations.
- **Customization:** Businesses can tailor infrastructure to meet specific needs.
- **Regulatory Compliance:** Supports strict data governance and security policies.

Pros

✓ **Higher Security & Compliance:** Suitable for handling sensitive or classified data.

✓ **Greater Customization:** Organizations can configure their cloud environment as needed.

✓ **Predictable Performance:** No resource sharing with other entities ensures consistent performance.

Cons

✗ **Higher Costs:** Requires significant upfront investment and ongoing maintenance.

✗ **Complex Management:** IT teams must handle maintenance, updates, and security measures.

Examples of Private Cloud Solutions

- **VMware Cloud** – Enterprise-level private cloud solutions for businesses.
- **OpenStack** – An open-source private cloud platform for customized deployments.

3. Hybrid Cloud

A **hybrid cloud** is a combination of **public and private cloud environments**, allowing businesses to **leverage the advantages of both models**. Organizations can store sensitive data in a private cloud while using the public cloud for high-volume workloads, achieving a balance between **security, scalability, and cost-efficiency**.

Key Features

- **Workload Optimization:** Different workloads can run in different environments based on performance and security needs.
- **Seamless Data Integration:** Secure data movement between private and public clouds.

- **Cost Efficiency:** Businesses can minimize costs by keeping critical workloads private and using the public cloud for less-sensitive operations.

Pros

✓ **Greater Flexibility:** Allows businesses to choose where to host workloads.

✓ **Cost Savings:** Reduces infrastructure costs by leveraging public cloud resources.

✓ **Optimized Performance:** Ensures that sensitive data is kept secure while taking advantage of public cloud scalability.

Cons

✗ **Complex Management:** Requires integration between public and private cloud environments.

✗ **Security Challenges:** Data movement between clouds must be secured to prevent breaches.

Use Cases

- **Financial Institutions:** Storing customer data in a private cloud while running analytics on a public cloud.
- **E-commerce Platforms:** Handling sensitive transactions in a private cloud and using the public cloud for customer-facing services.

4. Multi-Cloud

A **multi-cloud** strategy involves using **multiple cloud providers** to avoid vendor lock-in, improve redundancy, and enhance performance. Instead of relying on a single cloud provider, businesses **distribute workloads across multiple clouds**, selecting services that best fit their needs.

Key Features

- **Vendor Independence:** Reduces reliance on a single provider, increasing flexibility.
- **Enhanced Reliability:** If one cloud provider experiences downtime, another can take over operations.
- **Best-of-Breed Solutions:** Allows businesses to choose the best cloud services for specific applications.

Pros

✓ **Avoids Vendor Lock-In:** Greater control over pricing, features, and performance.

✓ **Increased Redundancy:** Enhances availability and disaster recovery.

✓ **Optimized Cost & Performance:** Businesses can mix and match cloud services to suit their needs.

Cons

✗ **Complex Management:** Requires expertise to integrate and secure multiple cloud environments.

✗ **Security Risks:** Managing multiple providers increases the attack surface and requires strong security policies.

Use Cases

- **Global Enterprises:** Distributing workloads across different regions using multiple cloud providers.
- **AI & Machine Learning Workloads:** Utilizing cloud-specific AI capabilities from different vendors.
- **Disaster Recovery & Business Continuity:** Ensuring high availability by spreading resources across clouds.

Choosing the Right Cloud Deployment Model

The choice of **public, private, hybrid, or multi-cloud** environments depends on an organization's needs for **security, cost, control, and flexibility:**

Cloud Model	Best For	Key Benefits	Challenges
Public Cloud	Startups, enterprises, SaaS providers	Cost-effective, scalable, no infrastructure management	Less control over security and compliance
Private Cloud	Regulated industries, enterprises with sensitive data	High security, compliance, and customization	Expensive, requires in-house expertise
Hybrid Cloud	Businesses needing flexibility between security and scalability	Optimized performance, cost efficiency, flexibility	Complex integration and management
Multi-Cloud	Large enterprises,	Best-of-breed solutions,	Complex security and

	businesses avoiding vendor lock-in	redundancy, performance optimization	administration

Organizations should assess their **data security needs, compliance regulations, and budget constraints** before adopting a cloud model. While the **public cloud** is ideal for cost-conscious businesses, the **private cloud** suits those prioritizing security. Meanwhile, **hybrid and multi-cloud** approaches provide a balance between **flexibility, performance, and risk management.**

Key Cloud Service Providers: AWS, Azure, Google Cloud

Cloud computing has revolutionized the way businesses manage their IT infrastructure, providing scalable, flexible, and cost-effective solutions. Several cloud providers dominate the market, each offering unique services tailored to different business needs. The three leading cloud service providers—**Amazon Web Services (AWS), Microsoft Azure, and Google Cloud Platform (GCP)**—offer a vast range of cloud computing capabilities, including compute power, storage, networking, artificial intelligence (AI), and data analytics.

1. Amazon Web Services (AWS)

Overview

Amazon Web Services (AWS) is the world's leading cloud computing platform, offering an extensive suite of cloud services that cater to businesses of all sizes. Launched by **Amazon in 2006**, AWS has established itself as the **largest and most widely adopted cloud provider**, serving industries such as **finance, healthcare, gaming, and government sectors**. AWS provides a robust, secure, and scalable infrastructure that enables organizations to run workloads efficiently, whether they need virtual servers, AI/ML tools, or IoT services.

Key Features

AWS offers a diverse range of services, with some of the most widely used including:

- **Amazon EC2 (Elastic Compute Cloud):** Virtual servers for running applications.
- **Amazon S3 (Simple Storage Service):** Scalable object storage for data backup and retrieval.
- **AWS Lambda:** Serverless computing service for running event-driven applications without managing infrastructure.
- **Amazon SageMaker:** A powerful AI and machine learning platform that enables businesses to build, train, and deploy models at scale.
- **Amazon RDS (Relational Database Service):** Managed relational database services supporting MySQL, PostgreSQL, and SQL Server.

AI Services in AWS

- **Amazon SageMaker:** Provides tools for building, training, and deploying machine learning models.
- **AWS DeepLens:** AI-powered deep learning-enabled camera for computer vision applications.
- **Amazon Lex:** Conversational AI service for building chatbots and voice assistants.
- **Amazon Rekognition:** Image and video analysis for facial recognition, object detection, and scene analysis.

- **AWS Comprehend:** Natural language processing (NLP) service for text analysis and sentiment detection.

Strengths of AWS

✓ **Global Infrastructure:** AWS has the **largest cloud infrastructure footprint**, with data centers in multiple regions worldwide.

✓ **Comprehensive Services:** Offers **over 200 cloud services**, covering computing, storage, AI, databases, IoT, and security.

✓ **Enterprise-Grade Security:** AWS provides **strong security frameworks**, including compliance with standards such as **ISO 27001, HIPAA, and GDPR**.

✓ **Strong AI & ML Capabilities:** With services like **SageMaker**, AWS is a leader in AI/ML innovation.

Considerations

✗ **Pricing Complexity:** AWS pricing can be challenging to navigate due to its **pay-as-you-go model** with multiple pricing tiers.

✗ **Steep Learning Curve:** The vast number of services and configurations can be overwhelming for beginners.

2. Microsoft Azure

Overview

Microsoft Azure is a leading cloud service provider, known for its seamless integration with **Microsoft products** such as **Windows Server, Active Directory, and Microsoft 365**. Azure is the preferred choice for enterprises that rely on Microsoft technologies and want to leverage hybrid cloud capabilities. Azure provides a range of solutions for businesses, developers, and IT professionals, supporting **AI, IoT, big data, and hybrid cloud** implementations.

Key Features

Azure's ecosystem includes numerous cloud solutions, with key offerings such as:

- **Azure Virtual Machines (VMs):** Scalable virtual computing resources for running applications.
- **Azure Kubernetes Service (AKS):** Fully managed Kubernetes for containerized applications.
- **Azure AI & Cognitive Services:** AI-driven tools for natural language processing, image recognition, and speech-to-text capabilities.
- **Azure Blob Storage:** Object storage for unstructured data, similar to AWS S3.
- **Azure Synapse Analytics:** A powerful analytics service for big data and business intelligence.

AI Services in Azure

- **Azure Machine Learning:** A comprehensive platform for building, training, and deploying AI models.
- **Azure Cognitive Services:** Provides pre-built AI models for vision, speech, language, and decision-making tasks.
- **Azure Bot Services:** Enables the development of intelligent chatbots.

- **Azure Computer Vision:** Image and video recognition with face and object detection capabilities.
- **Azure Speech Services:** Text-to-speech and speech-to-text conversion with language translation features.

Strengths of Azure

✓ **Enterprise Adoption:** Azure is widely used in corporate environments due to its **tight integration with Microsoft products.**

✓ **Hybrid Cloud Capabilities:** Azure provides **seamless on-premises and cloud integration** through **Azure Arc and Azure Stack.**

✓ **Strong AI & ML Integration:** With tools like **Azure Machine Learning,** businesses can develop advanced AI models.

✓ **Security & Compliance:** Azure supports enterprise security standards and **government compliance regulations,** making it a top choice for **regulated industries.**

Considerations

✗ **Pricing Variability:** Costs can fluctuate depending on service usage and configurations.

✗ **Less Third-Party Integration:** While Azure is strong within the Microsoft ecosystem, it may not be as open to third-party integrations as AWS or GCP.

3. Google Cloud Platform (GCP)

Overview

Google Cloud Platform (GCP) is known for its **advanced data analytics, machine learning, and Kubernetes capabilities.** While not as dominant as AWS or Azure in enterprise adoption, **GCP excels in big data processing, AI, and open-source technologies**. Google's cloud services are particularly popular among tech companies, startups, and data-driven businesses.

Key Features

GCP provides a robust set of cloud computing services, with notable offerings including:

- **Compute Engine:** Virtual machines for scalable computing power.
- **BigQuery:** A **serverless data warehouse** for real-time analytics and data processing.
- **Vertex AI:** A fully managed machine learning platform for developing and deploying AI models.
- **Google Kubernetes Engine (GKE):** A leading **managed Kubernetes service**, supporting containerized applications.
- **Cloud Storage:** Object storage with **high availability and redundancy**.

AI Services in GCP

- **Vertex AI:** A unified AI platform for building and deploying machine learning models.
- **Cloud AI APIs:** Pre-trained models for vision, language, and structured data analysis.
- **Dialogflow:** Conversational AI for chatbots and virtual assistants.
- **AutoML:** Custom machine learning models for non-experts.

- **TensorFlow:** Open-source deep learning framework developed by Google.

Strengths of GCP

✔ **Data Analytics Leadership:** Google's **BigQuery** is one of the most powerful tools for big data analysis.

✔ **AI & Machine Learning Expertise:** GCP provides industry-leading **AI/ML services**, including **Google TensorFlow** for deep learning applications.

✔ **Open-Source & Kubernetes Leadership:** Google was the **original developer of Kubernetes**, making GKE one of the best container orchestration platforms.

✔ **Cost-Effective Pricing:** GCP often offers **competitive pricing**, particularly for AI and analytics workloads.

Considerations

✘ **Smaller Market Share:** Compared to AWS and Azure, GCP has **fewer enterprise customers** and a **smaller global presence**.

✘ **Limited Enterprise Focus:** While GCP is strong in AI and data analytics, **its business applications are less comprehensive than Azure**.

<u>**Choosing the Right Cloud Provider**</u>

The choice between **AWS, Azure, and Google Cloud** depends on business requirements, industry needs, and long-term strategy:

- **AWS** is ideal for organizations that need a **comprehensive cloud platform with global infrastructure** and **extensive service offerings**.
- **Azure** is best for enterprises that rely on **Microsoft products** and require strong **hybrid cloud solutions**.
- **Google Cloud** is the preferred choice for **AI, machine learning, and big data analytics**, especially for businesses leveraging **open-source technologies**.

Cloud Storage, Virtualization, and Scalability in AI

As cloud computing continues to evolve, it plays a critical role in enabling businesses to store, process, and scale data efficiently. **Cloud storage, virtualization, and scalability** are foundational elements that support modern computing environments, particularly in data-intensive fields like artificial intelligence (AI). These technologies provide organizations with the flexibility, efficiency, and cost-effectiveness needed to manage large-scale workloads while ensuring security, reliability, and accessibility.

1. Cloud Storage

Overview

Cloud storage is a technology that allows users to store, retrieve, and manage data remotely using **internet-based storage solutions** instead of relying on traditional on-premises hardware. Cloud storage providers offer a **pay-as-you-go** model, ensuring **scalability, durability, and redundancy** without the need for extensive physical infrastructure.

Types of Cloud Storage

Cloud storage comes in multiple forms, each catering to different use cases and performance needs:

1. **Object Storage**

o Designed for **unstructured data**, such as images, videos, backups, and big data analytics.

o Common services: **Amazon S3 (Simple Storage Service), Azure Blob Storage, Google Cloud Storage**.

o Best for: Large-scale data storage, backup solutions, and content delivery.

2. **Block Storage**

o Provides low-latency, high-performance storage that works like traditional **hard drives**.

o Common services: **Amazon EBS (Elastic Block Store), Azure Managed Disks, Google Persistent Disks**.

o Best for: **Databases, transactional applications, and high-performance workloads**.

3. **File Storage**

o Supports **hierarchical file structures**, similar to network file systems (NFS).

o Common services: **Google Cloud Filestore, AWS FSx, Azure Files**.

o Best for: **Enterprise applications, shared file storage, and collaborative environments**.

Advantages of Cloud Storage

✓ **Scalability** – Automatically expands to accommodate growing data needs.

✓ **Cost-Efficiency** – Pay only for the storage used, reducing infrastructure costs.

✓ **High Availability & Reliability** – Data is distributed across multiple locations, minimizing downtime.

✓ **Security & Compliance** – Cloud storage providers implement **encryption, access controls, and compliance standards** (e.g., GDPR, HIPAA).

Challenges in Cloud Storage

✗ **Data Transfer Costs** – Moving large amounts of data in and out of the cloud can be expensive.

✗ **Latency Issues** – Accessing large datasets from remote storage may introduce delays.

✗ **Security Concerns** – Storing sensitive data requires **strong encryption and access management.**

2. Virtualization

Overview

Virtualization is the **key technology behind cloud computing**, allowing multiple **virtual environments** to run on a **single physical machine.** This is achieved using **hypervisors**, which abstract and allocate physical resources (CPU, memory, storage) to **virtual machines (VMs) or containers.**

Types of Virtualization

1. **Server Virtualization**
   o Divides a physical server into multiple **virtual servers** (VMs) with dedicated resources.
   o Used in **AWS EC2, Azure Virtual Machines, and Google Compute Engine.**
2. **Storage Virtualization**
   o Combines multiple physical storage devices into a **single, centralized storage pool.**

     o Used in **AWS Elastic Block Store (EBS) and Azure Storage Spaces.**

3. **Network Virtualization**
     o Abstracts network resources, enabling **software-defined networking (SDN).**
     o Used in **Azure Virtual Network (VNet), AWS VPC, and Google Cloud VPC.**

Benefits of Virtualization

✓ **Resource Optimization** – Maximizes **hardware utilization** by running multiple applications on a single server.

✓ **Cost Savings** – Reduces the need for expensive **on-premises infrastructure.**

✓ **Improved Reliability** – Virtual environments can be backed up, migrated, and restored quickly.

✓ **Faster Deployment** – Allows for rapid provisioning of **virtual machines, containers, and microservices.**

Challenges of Virtualization

✗ **Performance Overhead** – Virtualization introduces additional layers, which can slightly reduce performance.

✗ **Security Risks** – If **one VM is compromised,** others running on the same host could be affected.

✗ **Complexity in Management** – Requires **robust orchestration tools** like Kubernetes and VMware vSphere.

3. Scalability in AI

Overview

Scalability is **critical for AI workloads,** as AI models often require **large amounts of data** and **high computational power.** Scalability ensures that cloud infrastructure can dynamically **increase or decrease resources** based on workload demands, optimizing performance and cost-efficiency.

Types of Scalability

1. **Vertical Scaling (Scaling Up)**
   - o **Increases computing power** by adding more **CPU, RAM, or GPU** to an existing machine.
   - o Best for: **AI model training, deep learning frameworks, and high-performance applications.**
   - o Example: Upgrading an **AWS EC2 instance** from **m5.large to m5.2xlarge.**
2. **Horizontal Scaling (Scaling Out)**
   - o **Adds more machines** (instances or nodes) to handle increasing workloads.
   - o Best for: **Distributed AI workloads, big data processing, and microservices-based architectures.**
   - o Example: Deploying multiple AI inference nodes across **Google Kubernetes Engine (GKE).**

Challenges of Scaling AI Workloads

✘ **Cost Management** – Scaling AI requires **high-performance GPUs and TPUs,** increasing cloud costs.

✘ **Workload Balancing** – Ensuring efficient **load distribution** across multiple nodes is complex.

✗ **Latency Issues** – AI models require **low-latency responses**, especially in real-time applications like autonomous vehicles or fraud detection.

Cloud Solutions for AI Scalability

- **AWS:** Uses **Elastic Load Balancer (ELB), Auto Scaling Groups (ASG), and AWS Inferentia (AI accelerators).**
- **Azure:** Offers **Azure Machine Learning, Autoscale, and Azure Batch for parallel AI processing**.
- **Google Cloud:** Provides **TPUs (Tensor Processing Units) and Vertex AI for scalable AI workloads.**

Summary

Cloud computing serves as the backbone of modern technology, providing scalable, secure, and flexible computing environments. Understanding the fundamentals of cloud computing, including its service models, deployment environments, and major cloud providers, is essential for leveraging its full potential. The integration of cloud storage, virtualization, and scalability plays a critical role in supporting AI-driven solutions, ensuring businesses can harness the power of AI efficiently. As cloud computing continues to evolve, it will further enhance AI capabilities, shaping the future of intelligent automation and innovation.

Part 2: AI in Cloud Computing – Integration and Impact

Chapter 4: AI-Enabled Cloud Services

Introduction

As organizations increasingly adopt cloud computing, the integration of Artificial Intelligence (AI) into cloud services has transformed the way businesses operate. AI enhances cloud capabilities by improving automation, security, cost-efficiency, and scalability. This chapter explores the various AI-powered cloud service models, including SaaS, PaaS, and IaaS, along with their benefits, challenges, and practical applications. Additionally, we will examine AI-driven cloud security solutions, intelligent cloud monitoring, and AI-based cost optimization strategies.

AI-Powered SaaS, PaaS, and IaaS Offerings

Artificial Intelligence (AI) is transforming cloud computing by enhancing Software as a Service (SaaS), Platform as a Service (PaaS), and Infrastructure as a Service (IaaS). AI-driven cloud solutions are enabling businesses to optimize operations, improve decision-making, and enhance user experiences through automation and advanced analytics. From AI-powered **customer relationship management (CRM) systems** to **intelligent cloud infrastructure management**, AI plays a crucial role in every cloud service model.

1. AI in Software as a Service (SaaS)

SaaS applications leverage AI to provide **intelligent automation, predictive analytics, and personalized experiences** across various industries. Businesses use AI-powered SaaS solutions to **enhance customer engagement, improve business intelligence, and**

streamline workflows. These applications **eliminate the need for on-premises software installations** and offer **scalability, cost-efficiency, and real-time data processing.**

One of the most prominent AI-driven SaaS applications is **AI-powered Customer Relationship Management (CRM).** Platforms such as **Salesforce Einstein** utilize AI for **predictive lead scoring, automated customer interactions, and sentiment analysis,** enabling organizations to enhance customer relationships and improve sales forecasting. Similarly, **AI-driven Business Intelligence (BI) platforms,** like **Microsoft Power BI and Google Looker,** use AI algorithms to analyze vast amounts of data, uncover hidden patterns, and generate actionable insights without requiring extensive manual effort.

AI is also revolutionizing **content management and automation.** Solutions like **Adobe Sensei** use AI to **automate image tagging, enhance video editing, and generate intelligent design recommendations.** AI-driven SaaS offerings in content management help businesses create engaging content efficiently while ensuring **consistency and accuracy** across platforms.

By integrating AI, SaaS applications become **smarter and more adaptive,** allowing businesses to **reduce operational costs, increase productivity, and offer enhanced user experiences** through automated decision-making and intelligent recommendations.

2. AI in Platform as a Service (PaaS)

PaaS solutions enable developers to **build, deploy, and manage applications** without worrying about the underlying infrastructure. AI-powered PaaS enhances this experience by **simplifying development processes, improving scalability, and automating complex workflows.** With AI integration, PaaS solutions help businesses develop **intelligent applications faster and more efficiently.**

One major AI-powered PaaS offering is **Machine Learning as a Service (MLaaS)**. Cloud providers such as **AWS SageMaker, Google AI Platform, and Azure Machine Learning** allow developers to **train, deploy, and scale machine learning models** without requiring extensive AI expertise. These platforms provide **pre-built AI models, automated data preprocessing, and hyperparameter tuning**, reducing the complexity of AI development.

AI also plays a crucial role in **database management** within PaaS environments. AI-driven databases utilize **machine learning algorithms to optimize query performance, automate indexing, and enhance security**. Cloud services like **Google BigQuery and Amazon Aurora** incorporate AI to predict workload patterns, dynamically allocate resources, and detect potential security threats before they escalate.

Another key area where AI enhances PaaS is **serverless computing**. AI-driven **Functions-as-a-Service (FaaS)**, such as **AWS Lambda and Azure Functions**, allow developers to **execute code in response to triggers without managing servers**. These AI-driven functions optimize execution efficiency, automatically scale workloads, and enable real-time data processing.

By integrating AI, PaaS solutions **empower businesses with intelligent automation, improve resource utilization, and accelerate AI-driven innovation**, making them essential for modern application development.

3. AI in Infrastructure as a Service (IaaS)

IaaS provides **on-demand computing, storage, and networking resources**, allowing businesses to run applications without investing in physical hardware. AI enhances IaaS by **optimizing resource management, improving network performance, predicting** infrastructure failures, ensuring **higher efficiency, and reduced operational costs.**

One of the most significant AI-driven advancements in IaaS is **AI-powered cloud orchestration.** Cloud providers like **AWS, Azure, and Google Cloud** use AI algorithms to **automate provisioning, load balancing, and auto-scaling** of virtual machines, ensuring that cloud resources are efficiently allocated based on real-time demands. This minimizes wasted resources and helps businesses control costs while maintaining **optimal performance.**

AI also enhances **network optimization** within IaaS environments. AI-powered services like **AWS Global Accelerator** analyze network traffic patterns in real-time and optimize **data routing to reduce latency** and improve application responsiveness. Similarly, **Google Cloud's AI-driven network intelligence** identifies potential network bottlenecks and automatically reroutes traffic to prevent downtime.

Another critical AI-driven capability in IaaS is **predictive maintenance.** AI models analyze infrastructure health metrics to **detect hardware failures, forecast potential outages, and recommend preventive actions** before disruptions occur. This is particularly beneficial for large-scale cloud environments, where maintaining uptime and system reliability is crucial.

By leveraging AI, IaaS providers can **offer smarter, self-healing infrastructure that dynamically adjusts to workloads, reduces manual intervention, and ensures cost-effective cloud resource management.**

AI-Based Cloud Security Solutions

As cyber threats become more sophisticated, organizations are increasingly relying on **AI-powered security solutions** to protect sensitive data and prevent cyberattacks in the cloud. Traditional security measures often struggle to keep up with the sheer volume and complexity of modern threats. AI-driven security solutions enhance **threat detection, automated response, and identity management**, making cloud environments more resilient to cyber risks.

1. Threat Detection and Prevention

AI-driven **threat detection and prevention** solutions use advanced machine learning algorithms to analyze vast amounts of security data in real-time. These systems identify patterns, detect anomalies, and predict potential threats before they cause significant damage.

Security platforms like **Microsoft Defender for Cloud and AWS GuardDuty** leverage **AI-driven threat intelligence** to monitor cloud environments continuously. These tools use machine learning to differentiate between normal and suspicious activities, flagging potential security breaches such as **unauthorized access attempts, unusual data transfers, and malware infections**.

Another crucial aspect of AI-driven security is **User Behavior Analytics (UBA)**. AI-based UBA solutions analyze user actions and detect anomalies that may indicate **insider threats, compromised credentials, or suspicious login attempts**. For example, if a user suddenly accesses sensitive data from an unusual location or at an atypical time, AI-powered security systems can **trigger alerts, request additional authentication, or automatically block access** to prevent potential breaches.

By utilizing **predictive analytics and automated threat intelligence**, AI-powered threat detection solutions significantly **reduce response times, minimize false positives, and enhance overall cloud security posture**.

2. Automated Incident Response

AI-driven **automated incident response** enables organizations to **detect, analyze, and remediate security incidents** in real-time. Cyberattacks can happen within seconds, making manual intervention ineffective in mitigating threats swiftly. AI-powered security solutions use **predefined response mechanisms** to neutralize threats **before they escalate**.

AI-driven **Security Information and Event Management (SIEM)** solutions, such as **Splunk and IBM QRadar**, enhance **threat intelligence and security monitoring** by correlating data from multiple sources. These platforms use **AI and machine learning** to identify attack patterns, prioritize alerts based on severity, and initiate automated remediation actions. For instance, if AI detects a **ransomware attack**, the system can **immediately isolate the affected server, block malicious IP addresses, and notify security teams**, reducing potential damage.

Another critical AI-powered security feature is **automated security orchestration and response (SOAR)**. AI-driven SOAR platforms integrate with various security tools to **automate workflows, streamline threat investigation, and accelerate remediation efforts**. By automating tasks such as **log analysis, malware detection, and vulnerability patching**, AI helps security teams focus on more complex threats while ensuring **faster response times and improved accuracy**.

With AI-driven incident response, organizations can achieve **proactive security** rather than reactive measures, **reducing downtime, minimizing security risks, and enhancing overall cloud resilience**.

3. AI-Powered Identity and Access Management (IAM)

Managing identities and access controls in cloud environments is a complex challenge. AI-powered **Identity and Access Management**

(IAM) solutions enhance security by **analyzing user behavior, detecting anomalies, and enforcing adaptive authentication mechanisms.**

Traditional IAM systems rely on **static authentication rules**, which can be easily bypassed by cybercriminals. AI strengthens IAM by using **behavioral analytics and risk-based authentication** to determine whether a login attempt is legitimate. If AI detects **unusual access patterns**, such as multiple failed login attempts from different locations, it can **trigger multi-factor authentication (MFA), request biometric verification, or restrict access altogether.**

AI-driven biometric authentication is also transforming cloud security. Advanced **facial recognition, voice authentication, and fingerprint scanning** powered by AI enable organizations to implement **frictionless yet highly secure authentication mechanisms.** These AI-driven authentication methods **reduce reliance on passwords**, which are often compromised, and ensure that only authorized users can access sensitive cloud resources.

Additionally, AI-powered IAM solutions help organizations **enforce the principle of least privilege (PoLP) by dynamically adjusting user permissions based on real-time risk assessments.** For instance, AI can **automatically revoke unnecessary access rights, flag inactive user accounts, and monitor privileged user activities**, ensuring **strict access controls and regulatory compliance.**

By integrating AI with IAM, organizations can achieve **stronger authentication, reduced insider threats, and a seamless yet secure user experience**, ultimately enhancing overall cloud security.

Intelligent Cloud Monitoring and Management

As cloud environments become increasingly complex, businesses rely on **AI-driven cloud monitoring and management** solutions to enhance performance, reliability, and compliance. Traditional monitoring tools often generate vast amounts of data, making it challenging for IT teams to manually analyze and respond to performance issues. AI-powered monitoring tools use **machine learning, automation, and predictive analytics** to optimize cloud operations, ensuring **efficient resource utilization and proactive incident management**.

1. AI for Performance Monitoring

AI-driven **performance monitoring** solutions play a crucial role in maintaining **cloud efficiency and uptime**. These tools continuously analyze cloud environments to detect **performance bottlenecks, latency issues, and resource constraints**, helping businesses maintain seamless operations.

AI-based observability tools, such as **Datadog, New Relic, and Dynatrace**, provide **real-time insights** into cloud performance, tracking **CPU usage, memory consumption, network traffic, and database response times**. By leveraging **machine learning algorithms**, these tools **identify anomalies, predict potential failures, and suggest performance optimizations** before issues escalate.

Additionally, AI-powered performance monitoring tools help businesses **automate workload balancing** by dynamically adjusting **compute, storage, and networking resources** to meet demand fluctuations. This results in **reduced downtime, improved user experience, and optimized cost efficiency**.

By incorporating **AI-driven monitoring solutions**, organizations can ensure their cloud applications run smoothly while minimizing manual intervention, reducing operational costs, and enhancing overall system reliability.

2. Predictive Analytics for Cloud Operations

One of the most valuable applications of AI in cloud management is **predictive analytics**, which allows businesses to **anticipate and prevent system failures before they occur.** Traditional cloud monitoring tools react to performance issues **after** they happen, whereas AI-powered predictive analytics **identifies patterns, detects anomalies, and forecasts potential failures** in advance.

AI-based predictive analytics solutions analyze **historical performance data, workload trends, and system behavior** to predict **resource utilization, potential outages, and infrastructure inefficiencies.** For instance, AI can forecast **when servers will reach their capacity limits**, allowing organizations to **scale resources proactively and avoid performance degradation.**

Furthermore, **AI-driven anomaly detection** helps cloud teams identify irregular patterns in **network traffic, system logs, and application performance.** If AI detects **unusual spikes in resource consumption or potential security threats**, it can automatically trigger **alerts, initiate corrective actions, or even shut down affected instances** to prevent damage.

By leveraging **AI-powered predictive analytics**, organizations can **optimize cloud infrastructure planning, reduce unplanned downtime, and improve overall system resilience,** leading to enhanced business continuity and cost savings.

3. Autonomous Cloud Management

AI-driven **autonomous cloud management** takes automation a step further by **handling routine cloud operations** without human intervention. AI automates critical cloud management tasks such as **patching, backup, security updates, and resource scaling**, reducing the burden on IT teams while ensuring high availability.

For instance, AI-powered **self-healing cloud systems** can automatically detect and fix software bugs, apply security patches, and optimize database performance **without disrupting operations**. This automation enhances **cloud security and compliance** by **ensuring that all services remain up-to-date and protected from vulnerabilities**.

AI-driven **chatbots and virtual assistants** further enhance cloud management by providing **automated support and troubleshooting**. These AI-powered assistants help IT teams **diagnose system issues, recommend solutions, and even execute fixes** based on predefined rules. Tools like **Azure AI-based support agents and AWS Chatbot** integrate with cloud environments, enabling businesses to resolve cloud issues faster and more efficiently.

By implementing **autonomous cloud management**, organizations benefit from **reduced operational costs, faster incident resolution, and improved cloud efficiency**, allowing IT teams to focus on strategic initiatives rather than routine maintenance.

AI-Driven Cost Optimization in Cloud

As organizations increasingly rely on cloud services, managing cloud costs effectively has become a top priority. **AI-driven cost optimization** solutions help businesses **reduce unnecessary expenses, improve resource allocation, and predict future expenditures** with precision. By leveraging AI and machine learning, businesses can **maximize cloud efficiency, automate cost-saving strategies, and avoid budget overruns**.

1. Smart Resource Allocation

One of the primary ways AI optimizes cloud costs is through **smart resource allocation**, ensuring that cloud resources are used **efficiently and only when needed**. AI-driven **autoscaling mechanisms** dynamically adjust computing power based on real-time demand. For example, AI can **scale up resources** during peak usage periods and **scale down** when demand drops, preventing unnecessary expenses. This approach minimizes overprovisioning and ensures optimal performance without incurring additional costs.

Additionally, **AI-powered cost calculators**, such as **AWS Cost Explorer, Google Cloud Pricing Calculator, and Azure Cost Management,** provide **real-time insights** into cloud spending. These tools analyze **workload requirements, historical spending patterns, and service usage** to recommend **cost-saving measures** like switching to reserved instances or adjusting storage options. Businesses can use these AI-driven recommendations to **optimize cloud configurations and eliminate wasteful spending.**

By leveraging AI for **intelligent resource allocation**, organizations can **minimize idle resources, improve cost efficiency, and maintain cloud performance without excessive expenditure.**

2. AI for Cloud Cost Prediction

Cloud cost management is not just about reducing expenses but also about **forecasting future spending trends.** AI-powered **cost prediction models** analyze **historical usage patterns, billing trends, and workload fluctuations** to provide **accurate cost estimates.** These insights enable businesses to **plan budgets effectively, prevent unexpected cloud expenses, and allocate resources strategically.**

For example, AI-based forecasting tools can **predict seasonal spikes in cloud usage** and recommend proactive scaling strategies. Businesses with **e-commerce platforms, financial applications, or AI workloads** can use these insights to **adjust their cloud infrastructure in advance**, ensuring cost-effective scalability during high-demand periods.

Moreover, **AI-driven cost simulations** allow organizations to **model different cloud usage scenarios** before making deployment decisions. This helps **optimize pricing plans, choose cost-effective cloud instances, and implement workload scheduling strategies** that align with budgetary constraints.

By leveraging **AI for cloud cost prediction**, organizations gain **better financial control, improved budgeting accuracy, and reduced risks of unexpected cloud expenditures.**

3. AI-Based Waste Reduction

A significant portion of cloud expenses results from **underutilized or misconfigured resources,** leading to unnecessary spending. AI-driven **waste reduction strategies** help businesses **identify idle resources, optimize workloads, and recommend cost-effective configurations.**

AI-powered **rightsizing tools,** such as **AWS Compute Optimizer and Google Cloud Recommender,** analyze **CPU utilization, memory usage, and network performance** to suggest **the most appropriate cloud instance sizes.** These recommendations prevent businesses from **paying for oversized virtual machines (VMs) or underutilized storage services,** ensuring that workloads are aligned with actual resource needs.

Additionally, AI can **identify and terminate unused instances,** such as **zombie VMs, orphaned storage volumes, and idle databases,** which often go unnoticed and contribute to unnecessary cloud expenses. By automating **resource cleanup and optimization,** AI helps organizations **reduce cloud waste and maintain a cost-efficient infrastructure.**

Furthermore, AI-driven **workload scheduling** optimizes **non-essential tasks** (such as backups, batch processing, and testing environments) by running them **during off-peak hours when cloud**

pricing is lower. This approach significantly **lowers operational costs while maintaining performance standards**.

Through **AI-powered waste reduction techniques**, businesses can **eliminate redundant expenses, optimize cloud efficiency, and achieve long-term cost savings**.

Summary

AI-enabled cloud services are transforming businesses by enhancing automation, security, and cost efficiency. AI-powered SaaS, PaaS, and IaaS solutions provide intelligent capabilities for various applications, from customer relationship management to machine learning as a service. AI-driven security solutions strengthen cloud protection through threat detection, automated incident response, and identity management. Additionally, AI enhances cloud monitoring and management, ensuring optimal performance and reliability. Lastly, AI-driven cost optimization strategies help organizations minimize cloud expenses by predicting usage trends and eliminating waste. As AI continues to evolve, its role in cloud computing will only become more significant, enabling businesses to operate more efficiently and securely.

Chapter 5: Cloud Infrastructure for AI Workloads

Introduction

Cloud computing has revolutionized AI by providing scalable and flexible infrastructure for AI workloads. As AI applications demand significant computational power, cloud-based solutions offer the necessary resources to handle complex computations efficiently. This chapter explores how cloud computing enhances AI scalability, the role of specialized hardware like GPUs and TPUs, AI-optimized cloud platforms, and distributed AI processing.

How Cloud Computing Enhances AI Scalability

The fusion of **cloud computing and artificial intelligence (AI)** has revolutionized how businesses develop, deploy, and scale AI applications. AI workloads require vast amounts of **computational power, storage, and seamless integration with AI frameworks**, which cloud computing efficiently provides. Cloud-based AI solutions enable organizations to **scale dynamically, optimize resource usage, and drive innovation without the constraints of traditional on-premises infrastructure**.

1. On-Demand Compute Resources

One of the most significant advantages of cloud computing for AI scalability is its **on-demand compute resources**. AI applications—particularly those involving **deep learning, natural language processing (NLP), and computer vision**—demand high-performance computing power to process large datasets and execute complex algorithms.

With cloud platforms like **Amazon Web Services (AWS), Microsoft Azure, and Google Cloud Platform (GCP)**, businesses can **scale compute resources up or down based on real-time demand**. Instead of investing in expensive **on-premises GPUs, TPUs, and high-performance clusters**, organizations can leverage cloud-based solutions such as:

- **AWS EC2 instances (including GPU and FPGA-based instances)**
- **Azure Machine Learning Compute Clusters**
- **Google Cloud AI Platform with Tensor Processing Units (TPUs)**

These resources allow AI applications to **train models faster, execute large-scale data processing, and support real-time AI inference** without the hassle of managing physical infrastructure. Cloud-based compute elasticity ensures that AI projects remain **cost-effective, responsive to workload fluctuations, and capable of handling high computational demands efficiently**.

2. Elastic Storage Solutions

AI models rely heavily on vast amounts of data for **training, validation, and real-time inference**. Traditional on-premises storage solutions often struggle to handle the sheer volume of **structured and unstructured data** required for AI workloads. Cloud computing addresses this challenge through **scalable, flexible, and cost-efficient storage solutions**.

Cloud storage services, such as **Amazon S3, Google Cloud Storage, and Azure Blob Storage**, provide AI models with **elastic, high-speed**

access to data across distributed environments. These solutions offer:

- **Infinite scalability**: Cloud storage can expand as datasets grow, ensuring that AI applications never run out of space.
- **High availability and redundancy**: Data is automatically replicated across multiple data centers, reducing the risk of loss or downtime.
- **Seamless data retrieval**: AI models can fetch and process data on demand, optimizing performance for real-time analytics and inference.

Additionally, **cloud-based data lakes and data warehouses** (such as **Amazon Redshift, Google BigQuery, and Azure Synapse Analytics**) enable organizations to store and analyze massive datasets efficiently. These storage solutions allow AI models to **process terabytes or even petabytes of data** without latency issues, making them essential for **AI-driven big data analytics, predictive modeling, and machine learning automation**.

3. Seamless Integration with AI Frameworks

AI model development requires **robust frameworks and tools** to design, train, and deploy machine learning and deep learning models. Cloud computing simplifies this process by **offering pre-integrated AI frameworks, managed services, and end-to-end MLOps pipelines** that accelerate AI adoption.

Cloud platforms provide **native support** for industry-leading AI frameworks, including:

- **TensorFlow** (for deep learning and neural networks)
- **PyTorch** (for flexible AI model development)
- **Scikit-learn** (for classical machine learning algorithms)

- **Keras, MXNet, and Hugging Face Transformers** (for NLP and generative AI)

With **serverless AI services**, such as **AWS SageMaker, Google Vertex AI, and Azure Machine Learning**, developers can train, fine-tune, and deploy AI models without needing to manage underlying hardware. These platforms offer:

- **Prebuilt AI models and APIs** (for vision, speech, text, and recommendation systems)
- **Automated hyperparameter tuning** (for optimizing model performance)
- **End-to-end ML pipelines** (for seamless model training, validation, and deployment)

By leveraging **cloud-based AI frameworks**, businesses can significantly **reduce development time, enhance collaboration, and streamline model deployment across multiple environments**. Cloud integration eliminates infrastructure bottlenecks, allowing AI teams to focus on **innovation, experimentation, and rapid iteration**.

GPUs, TPUs, and High-Performance Computing (HPC) for AI

Artificial Intelligence (AI) and machine learning (ML) workloads demand **exceptional computational power** to process vast datasets, train complex models, and deliver real-time inference. Traditional **Central Processing Units (CPUs)**, while versatile, often lack the speed and efficiency required for deep learning and advanced AI applications. This is where specialized hardware—**Graphics Processing Units (GPUs), Tensor Processing Units (TPUs), and High-Performance Computing (HPC) clusters**—becomes essential. These technologies **accelerate AI computations, optimize deep learning performance, and enable large-scale AI model training**.

1. Graphics Processing Units (GPUs)

GPUs have become the backbone of AI development due to their ability to **parallelize computations**. Unlike CPUs, which are optimized for sequential processing, GPUs are designed to handle thousands of **simultaneous operations**. This makes them particularly well-suited for:

- **Deep Learning Model Training**: GPUs speed up training processes by distributing computations across multiple cores.
- **Computer Vision and Image Recognition**: AI models analyzing images or video streams benefit from the high throughput of GPUs.
- **Natural Language Processing (NLP)**: Large language models (LLMs) such as **GPT and BERT** require immense parallel computing power, which GPUs efficiently provide.

Popular GPU Solutions for AI

Leading cloud providers offer GPU-accelerated computing services tailored for AI workloads:

- **NVIDIA A100 and H100 GPUs** (widely used for AI and ML acceleration).
- **AWS GPU Instances** (P3, P4, and G5 instances for deep learning training and inference).
- **Google Cloud GPUs** (supporting **TensorFlow, PyTorch, and JAX** for AI model development).
- **Azure NV-Series VMs** (optimized for AI and high-performance graphics applications).

By leveraging GPUs in cloud environments, businesses can **reduce training times, enhance model efficiency, and scale AI solutions effortlessly.**

2. Tensor Processing Units (TPUs)

Tensor Processing Units (TPUs) are **custom AI accelerators** developed by Google, specifically optimized for deep learning tasks. Unlike GPUs, TPUs are **designed for matrix multiplications**—a fundamental operation in deep learning algorithms.

Advantages of TPUs in AI

- **High-Speed Matrix Operations**: TPUs process large batches of data more efficiently than traditional hardware.
- **Optimized for TensorFlow**: As part of Google's AI ecosystem, TPUs integrate seamlessly with **TensorFlow**, one of the most widely used deep learning frameworks.
- **Cost-Effective Training and Inference**: Compared to GPUs, TPUs can reduce AI model training costs while maintaining high computational efficiency.

TPU Use Cases

TPUs are particularly beneficial for AI workloads involving:

- **Large-Scale Deep Learning Models**: Google's TPUs power **BERT, T5, and other transformer-based NLP models**.
- **Autonomous Systems**: AI-driven robotics and self-driving technologies leverage TPUs for rapid decision-making.
- **Real-Time AI Inference**: TPUs accelerate cloud-based AI inference, making them ideal for **voice assistants, search engines, and AI-driven recommendations**.

Cloud TPU Services

Google Cloud offers **Cloud TPU v4 Pods**, which provide **unprecedented scalability for AI model training**. These TPUs help companies like OpenAI, DeepMind, and Google Research **train large AI models efficiently while minimizing energy consumption.**

3. High-Performance Computing (HPC) for AI

High-Performance Computing (HPC) combines multiple **high-speed processors, GPUs, and interconnected systems** to tackle computationally intensive AI tasks. AI applications that require vast amounts of **data processing, simulation, and predictive modeling** benefit significantly from HPC clusters.

Key Benefits of HPC for AI

- **Faster AI Model Training**: HPC clusters can train deep learning models across thousands of nodes, reducing training times from weeks to hours.
- **Scalability for AI Research**: Academic institutions, pharmaceutical companies, and financial firms leverage HPC for **complex simulations, drug discovery, and risk modeling.**
- **AI-Powered Scientific Discovery**: Supercomputers utilizing HPC enhance research in fields such as **genomics, climate modeling, and astrophysics.**

HPC Solutions in Cloud Computing

Cloud providers offer HPC services tailored for AI workloads:

- **AWS ParallelCluster** (manages and scales HPC clusters in AWS).
- **Azure HPC VMs** (optimized for AI training, simulations, and high-speed networking).
- **Google Cloud HPC** (accelerates AI and ML workloads with powerful compute clusters).

By integrating HPC with AI, businesses and research institutions can **unlock new possibilities, push computational limits, and accelerate AI-driven innovations.**

AI-Optimized Cloud Platforms: AWS SageMaker, Google AI Platform, and Azure Machine Learning

As artificial intelligence (AI) continues to revolutionize industries, cloud providers have developed specialized platforms to streamline **machine learning (ML) development, deployment, and scaling.** These AI-optimized cloud platforms offer **pre-built AI services, automated workflows, and scalable computing power,** allowing businesses to harness AI without managing complex infrastructure.

Three of the leading AI cloud platforms—**AWS SageMaker, Google AI Platform, and Azure Machine Learning (Azure ML)**—provide **end-to-end solutions** for training, deploying, and managing AI models. Each platform offers **unique capabilities** tailored to different AI use cases, from deep learning applications to automated model optimization.

1. AWS SageMaker: Fully Managed Machine Learning at Scale

Amazon SageMaker is a **fully managed AI service** that enables developers and data scientists to build, train, and deploy machine learning models **at scale.** By automating many aspects of the ML workflow, SageMaker reduces **development complexity, accelerates time to market, and optimizes model performance.**

Key Features of AWS SageMaker

- **Pre-Built Algorithms & AutoML**: SageMaker provides built-in machine learning algorithms and **AutoML capabilities** to simplify model training.

- **Distributed Training & Hyperparameter Tuning**: AI models can be trained across multiple GPUs, with automatic **hyperparameter optimization** for better accuracy.
- **SageMaker Studio**: An integrated development environment (IDE) for ML that includes **notebooks, data labeling, and model debugging tools.**
- **MLOps & Model Monitoring**: With features like **SageMaker Pipelines** for automation and **SageMaker Model Monitor** for drift detection, AWS ensures that models remain accurate over time.

Use Cases for AWS SageMaker

- **Fraud Detection**: Financial institutions use SageMaker to train fraud detection models that analyze **transaction patterns in real-time.**
- **Computer Vision**: Businesses leverage SageMaker for **image recognition, facial analysis, and defect detection** in manufacturing.
- **Natural Language Processing (NLP)**: Enterprises build AI-powered chatbots and sentiment analysis models using **pre-built NLP tools.**

By integrating seamlessly with **AWS cloud services like S3, Lambda, and EC2**, SageMaker allows businesses to **train and deploy AI models efficiently while reducing operational overhead.**

2. Google AI Platform: Scalable AI Development with Pre-Trained Models

Google AI Platform provides a **comprehensive suite of AI tools** that enable **model training, data analysis, and AI deployment** on Google Cloud. Designed to support **data scientists, researchers, and enterprises**, it integrates **Google's advanced AI infrastructure**, including **TensorFlow, Vertex AI, and AutoML.**

Key Features of Google AI Platform

- **AutoML & Pre-Trained Models**: Users can **train models with minimal coding** using **AutoML** or leverage **Google's pre-trained AI models** for tasks like image classification, speech recognition, and translation.
- **AI Infrastructure & TPUs**: The platform provides **GPU- and TPU-accelerated environments**, reducing the time required to train complex deep learning models.
- **Vertex AI Pipelines**: Enables **end-to-end AI workflow automation**, from data preprocessing to model deployment and monitoring.
- **BigQuery ML Integration**: Allows users to build and deploy ML models **directly within Google BigQuery**, eliminating the need for data movement.

Use Cases for Google AI Platform

- **Healthcare & Life Sciences**: AI-driven diagnostics and **predictive healthcare analytics** leverage Google's AI tools.
- **Retail & E-Commerce**: Businesses use Google AI for **personalized recommendations, inventory forecasting, and customer behavior analysis**.
- **Voice & Speech Recognition**: Google's AI services power applications like **Google Assistant, speech-to-text transcription, and voice-based authentication**.

With **native integrations** for Google's cloud ecosystem—**Cloud Storage, Kubernetes, and BigQuery**—Google AI Platform simplifies **large-scale AI deployments, making it ideal for businesses needing scalable AI solutions**.

3. Azure Machine Learning (Azure ML): Enterprise-Grade AI with Automated ML Tools

Azure Machine Learning (Azure ML) is Microsoft's **end-to-end AI development platform**, offering **automated AI tools, MLOps capabilities, and enterprise-grade security**. Built for **developers, data scientists, and AI engineers**, it supports **low-code and advanced AI development**.

Key Features of Azure ML

- **Automated Machine Learning (AutoML)**: Allows users to create high-performing models **without extensive coding** by automating feature selection, model selection, and hyperparameter tuning.
- **Azure ML Designer**: A **drag-and-drop interface** for building ML workflows, making AI accessible to non-experts.
- **Responsible AI Tools**: Includes **Fairness, Explainability, and Model Interpretability dashboards** to ensure **transparent and ethical AI**.
- **Azure MLOps**: Provides **continuous integration and continuous deployment (CI/CD)** for AI models, ensuring **scalability and reliability**.

Use Cases for Azure ML

- **Predictive Maintenance**: Manufacturing companies use **Azure ML for anomaly detection** and **failure prediction** in industrial equipment.
- **Financial Risk Assessment**: Banks leverage Azure ML to **identify fraudulent transactions, assess credit risk, and optimize investment strategies**.
- **Cybersecurity Threat Detection**: Enterprises deploy **AI-driven security models** to detect cyber threats and **enhance cloud security**.

With native integration into Microsoft's ecosystem—Azure Synapse, Power BI, and IoT Edge—Azure ML is an ideal AI platform for enterprises seeking scalable, compliant, and production-ready AI solutions.

Comparison of AI-Optimized Cloud Platforms

Feature	AWS SageMaker	Google AI Platform	Azure ML
Best For	AI model training & deployment at scale	AI research & AutoML solutions	Enterprise AI & automation
AutoML Support	Yes	Yes	Yes
Pre-Trained Models	Limited	Extensive (Google AI Hub)	Moderate
Infrastructure	GPU, EC2 instances	GPU, TPU-based computing	GPU, Azure Synapse
Workflow Automation	SageMaker Pipelines	Vertex AI Pipelines	Azure MLOps
Enterprise Security	Yes	Moderate	Strong (Compliance & Responsible AI)
Cloud Integration	AWS ecosystem	Google Cloud & BigQuery	Microsoft Azure & Power BI

Distributed AI Workloads and Serverless AI Processing

As AI models grow increasingly complex, the demand for **high-performance, scalable, and cost-efficient computing solutions** continues to rise. Cloud computing has revolutionized AI deployment by offering **distributed processing capabilities and serverless execution models**, enabling businesses to run AI workloads with greater efficiency and flexibility.

Distributed AI workloads allow AI models to be **processed across multiple cloud servers**, accelerating training times and optimizing performance. Meanwhile, serverless AI execution ensures that AI applications **run dynamically without requiring dedicated infrastructure management**, reducing operational overhead and optimizing costs.

1. Distributed AI Processing: Scaling AI Workloads Across Multiple Cloud Servers

AI models, particularly deep learning models, require **intensive computational power** to process vast amounts of data and train neural networks efficiently. Distributed AI processing leverages **cloud-based parallel computing** to split AI workloads across multiple machines, significantly reducing **training and inference times**.

Key Benefits of Distributed AI Processing

- **Accelerated AI Training**: By distributing training tasks across multiple GPUs, TPUs, or cloud servers, AI models can be trained **faster and more efficiently**.
- **Optimized Resource Utilization**: Cloud platforms dynamically allocate resources based on workload demands, ensuring **cost efficiency and high availability**.

- **Fault Tolerance & Reliability**: Distributed AI workloads provide **built-in redundancy,** ensuring **continuous operation even if some servers fail.**
- **Scalability for Large Datasets**: AI applications dealing with massive datasets—such as image recognition, natural language processing (NLP), and autonomous systems—benefit from **seamless scaling across multiple nodes.**

Distributed AI in Action: Use Cases

- **Autonomous Vehicles**: AI models processing real-time sensor data from self-driving cars **use distributed cloud computing to analyze data streams simultaneously.**
- **Healthcare & Genomics**: AI-driven genomic research distributes computations across cloud servers to **analyze DNA sequences at unprecedented speeds.**
- **Financial Forecasting**: AI models for stock market prediction utilize distributed processing to **analyze real-time market trends and simulate future scenarios.**
- **Computer Vision & Image Processing**: AI-powered facial recognition and object detection systems run distributed processing across cloud clusters for **high-speed inference and analysis.**

Major cloud providers, including **Google Cloud (TensorFlow Distributed Training), AWS (SageMaker Distributed Training), and Azure Machine Learning**, offer **pre-configured environments for distributed AI processing**, enabling enterprises to deploy and scale AI workloads seamlessly.

2. Serverless AI Execution: Running AI Models Without Infrastructure Management

Traditional AI deployments require **dedicated virtual machines (VMs), containers, or clusters**, often leading to **underutilized**

resources and increased operational complexity. Serverless computing eliminates these challenges by enabling AI applications to run on **demand-based execution models**, where compute resources are **provisioned automatically** and scale dynamically based on workload needs.

Key Advantages of Serverless AI Execution

- **Cost-Efficiency**: Serverless AI models **only consume resources when executed**, eliminating costs associated with idle infrastructure.
- **Automatic Scaling**: Cloud providers scale AI workloads **automatically**, ensuring that applications handle sudden spikes in demand **without manual intervention**.
- **Reduced Operational Overhead**: Developers can focus on AI model development rather than managing underlying infrastructure.
- **Event-Driven AI Processing**: Serverless platforms trigger AI functions based on real-time events, optimizing execution **for real-time analytics and decision-making**.

Serverless AI Services in Cloud Computing

Several cloud platforms offer **serverless AI execution environments**, allowing organizations to run AI workloads without managing infrastructure:

- **AWS Lambda**: Executes AI functions **in response to cloud events**, such as image uploads (triggering image recognition) or API requests (powering chatbots).
- **Google Cloud Functions**: Supports **serverless AI inference**, enabling AI-powered applications like **real-time speech translation and automated document processing**.

- **Azure Functions**: Runs AI-driven workloads **on demand**, integrating with Azure Cognitive Services for applications like **language understanding and anomaly detection.**

Serverless AI in Action: Use Cases

- **Chatbots & Virtual Assistants**: Serverless AI execution enables **real-time chatbot interactions** by processing user queries dynamically.
- **Fraud Detection**: AI models deployed in a serverless environment can **analyze transaction patterns and flag anomalies in real-time.**
- **Real-Time Video Analysis**: Serverless AI functions can process **live video streams**, detecting objects, faces, or suspicious activities without continuous infrastructure provisioning.
- **IoT & Edge Computing**: Serverless AI allows **AI-powered IoT devices to process data locally** and send results to the cloud for further analysis.

Comparison: Distributed AI vs. Serverless AI

Feature	Distributed AI Processing	Serverless AI Execution
Best For	Large-scale AI model training and real-time processing	Event-driven AI tasks and cost-efficient AI execution
Scalability	Horizontally scales across multiple servers	Automatically scales based on event triggers
Infrastructure Management	Requires cloud clusters and managed services	Fully managed by cloud providers (no infrastructure to manage)

Cost Model	Pay for allocated resources (even if underutilized)	Pay-per-use (only when functions execute)
Use Case Examples	Deep learning, genomics, financial forecasting, autonomous vehicles	Chatbots, real-time analytics, IoT, video processing

Summary

Cloud infrastructure plays a critical role in AI workloads by enabling scalable, cost-effective, and high-performance computing. Specialized hardware like GPUs, TPUs, and HPC enhances AI processing capabilities. AI-optimized cloud platforms provide tools for efficient model development and deployment, while distributed and serverless AI processing ensures optimal resource utilization. As AI continues to evolve, cloud computing will remain a cornerstone for AI-driven innovation.

Chapter 6: AI in Cloud Security and Compliance

Introduction

As cloud computing adoption grows, so do the complexities and risks associated with cloud security. Traditional security approaches struggle to keep up with the dynamic nature of cloud environments. Artificial Intelligence (AI) has emerged as a transformative force in cloud security, offering real-time threat detection, automated incident response, and enhanced compliance management. This chapter explores AI-powered threat detection and response, cloud-based Security Information and Event Management (SIEM), AI-driven data protection and encryption, and AI-based solutions for compliance challenges in cloud security.

AI-Powered Threat Detection and Response in the Cloud

As cyber threats become increasingly sophisticated, organizations are turning to **AI-driven security solutions** to detect, prevent, and respond to cyberattacks in real-time. Cloud security is no longer limited to traditional rule-based defenses; instead, AI-powered systems leverage **machine learning (ML), behavioral analytics, and automation** to enhance threat detection and incident response. These AI-driven capabilities allow security teams to **identify anomalies, mitigate risks, and orchestrate rapid responses** to potential security breaches.

1. AI for Threat Detection: Identifying and Preventing Cyber Threats in Real-time

AI-driven security solutions **continuously monitor cloud environments** to identify suspicious activities, detect anomalies, and prevent cyberattacks before they escalate. By utilizing **behavioral analytics and ML algorithms**, AI enhances cybersecurity by identifying patterns that may indicate security threats, such as unauthorized access, data exfiltration, or malware infiltration.

Key Components of AI-Based Threat Detection

Anomaly Detection: Recognizing Suspicious Activities

AI models analyze **network traffic, system logs, and user behavior** to detect deviations from normal activity. **Machine learning algorithms establish baselines** of typical behavior and flag any unusual patterns, such as:

- **Unusual Login Activity**: AI can detect unauthorized access attempts based on location, device, or time of access.
- **Data Exfiltration Attempts**: AI-based tools monitor outgoing data flows to detect unauthorized data transfers.
- **Lateral Movement Detection**: AI identifies suspicious internal movements that could indicate an attacker navigating through the network.

AI-Based Intrusion Detection Systems (IDS)

AI-driven **Intrusion Detection Systems (IDS)** enhance security by continuously monitoring network traffic and detecting **unauthorized access attempts**. Solutions such as **AWS GuardDuty, Azure Security Center, and Google Security Command Center** leverage AI to:

- **Detect Advanced Persistent Threats (APTs)** before they infiltrate cloud systems.
- **Analyze vast amounts of security logs** to correlate indicators of compromise (IoCs).
- **Prevent insider threats by analyzing privileged account behavior** for unauthorized access attempts.

Malware and Phishing Detection: Stopping Malicious Attacks

AI enhances traditional antivirus solutions by **detecting and blocking malware, ransomware, and phishing attacks** in real-time. AI-driven **email security and web filtering tools** scan:

- **Email Attachments and URLs**: AI scans incoming emails to detect and block phishing links and malicious file attachments.
- **Web Traffic and Downloads**: AI monitors user activity, blocking suspicious website access and preventing drive-by downloads.
- **File Integrity Monitoring**: AI analyzes file metadata and behavior to **detect fileless malware and zero-day threats**.

Cloud-native AI security solutions, such as **Microsoft Defender for Office 365, Google Safe Browsing, and Palo Alto Networks WildFire**, use AI models to identify **previously unseen threats** by analyzing patterns rather than relying on traditional signature-based detection.

2. AI-Driven Automated Incident Response: Rapid and Intelligent Threat Mitigation

Beyond detection, AI enhances **incident response by automating threat mitigation and security workflows**. Traditional security operations centers (SOCs) often face **alert fatigue**, with analysts manually investigating thousands of security alerts daily. AI-driven incident response tools **prioritize alerts, automate responses, and continuously adapt to new attack patterns**.

Automated Threat Mitigation: Reducing Human Intervention

AI-powered security tools **automate remediation actions** to neutralize threats **before they escalate**. Solutions like **Microsoft Defender, Google Chronicle, and AWS Security Hub** automatically:

- **Isolate compromised endpoints** to prevent malware spread.
- **Block malicious IPs, domains, and users** based on real-time threat intelligence.
- **Quarantine infected files and rollback system changes** to a safe state.

By reducing reliance on manual intervention, AI-driven security automation significantly decreases **response times and mitigates security risks faster**.

Self-Learning AI Security Systems: Adaptive Threat Protection

Unlike traditional security measures, **AI-based cybersecurity tools continuously evolve** by learning from new threats and refining their defense mechanisms. These self-learning AI security systems:

- **Analyze past incidents** to improve future threat detection.
- **Adapt to new attack techniques**, preventing zero-day exploits.
- **Reduce false positives** by fine-tuning threat detection models over time.

For example, **Darktrace's AI-driven cybersecurity platform** uses **self-learning AI to detect emerging threats and provide autonomous response capabilities** across cloud, network, and endpoint security layers.

AI-Driven Security Orchestration: Streamlining Incident Response Workflows

Security Orchestration, Automation, and Response (**SOAR**) platforms integrate AI with **automated playbooks** to streamline security operations. AI-driven SOAR solutions, such as **Splunk SOAR, IBM Resilient, and Palo Alto Cortex XSOAR**, enable security teams to:

- **Automate incident triage and investigation** by correlating security alerts.
- **Integrate threat intelligence sources** for faster decision-making.
- **Execute predefined security playbooks** to respond to threats automatically.

For instance, when AI detects an attempted **brute-force login attack**, a SOAR platform can **automatically block the attacker's IP, notify security teams, and escalate only critical alerts**, reducing manual workload.

Cloud-Based SIEM (Security Information and Event Management)

With the increasing adoption of cloud computing, organizations face **complex security challenges**, including **managing large volumes of security events, detecting sophisticated threats, and ensuring regulatory compliance**. Traditional on-premises SIEM solutions often struggle with **scalability and real-time analysis**, making **cloud-based SIEM solutions a necessity**. These solutions **centralize security data, enable proactive threat detection, and integrate AI-driven analytics** to improve security operations.

Cloud-based SIEM solutions aggregate security logs from **various cloud and on-premises sources**, including **network devices, firewalls, endpoints, and cloud services**. By leveraging **AI and machine**

learning, these platforms enhance threat detection, automate security responses, and provide deep visibility into an organization's security posture.

1. Role of SIEM in Cloud Security

Centralized Security Event Management

Cloud-based SIEM platforms provide a **unified view of security incidents** by **collecting, analyzing, and correlating logs** from multiple sources. This centralized approach helps security teams **monitor threats across distributed cloud environments** while ensuring compliance with **industry standards like GDPR, HIPAA, and ISO 27001**.

Real-Time Threat Correlation

Traditional SIEM solutions rely on **static rule-based alerts**, which often lead to **alert fatigue and overlooked threats**. AI-powered cloud SIEM solutions overcome this limitation by:

- **Analyzing large volumes of security logs in real-time** to detect anomalies and potential security breaches.
- Using **advanced correlation algorithms** to connect seemingly unrelated security events across multiple systems.
- Reducing **false positives** by applying machine learning techniques to differentiate between legitimate activities and actual threats.

For example, an AI-powered SIEM can **identify suspicious login attempts** from multiple geographic locations, correlate them with access patterns, and flag them as a potential **account compromise attack**.

AI-Driven Log Analysis

AI enhances SIEM log analysis by **automatically detecting unusual patterns and anomalies** in system logs. Traditional methods require **manual log reviews,** which can be time-consuming and prone to human error. AI-driven log analysis provides:

- **Automated anomaly detection** using behavior-based analytics.
- **Reduced false alarms** by learning from historical data and adjusting alert sensitivity.
- **Proactive threat identification** before attackers can exploit vulnerabilities.

For instance, if an employee's **behavior suddenly changes—such as accessing sensitive data at unusual hours**—AI-powered SIEM can **flag this as a potential insider threat.**

Predictive Threat Intelligence

Cloud-based SIEM platforms leverage AI to **predict and prevent future threats** by analyzing **historical security incidents** and identifying attack patterns. Predictive threat intelligence capabilities include:

- **Identifying trends in attack vectors** to anticipate emerging cyber threats.
- **Analyzing attacker behaviors** to strengthen security defenses.
- **Automating threat mitigation strategies** to prevent breaches before they occur.

For example, if an AI-driven SIEM detects **a pattern of phishing attempts targeting multiple employees,** it can **alert security teams** and recommend proactive measures, such as **blocking specific domains or implementing additional email security controls.**

2. Leading AI-Powered SIEM Solutions

Several cloud-based SIEM platforms **leverage AI and machine learning** to improve security operations. These solutions offer **advanced threat detection, automated responses, and seamless integration with cloud environments.**

IBM QRadar

IBM QRadar is an **AI-driven SIEM solution** designed to **automate threat detection and compliance monitoring**. It provides:

- **Behavior-based anomaly detection** using AI analytics.
- **Automated security alerts** to reduce manual intervention.
- **Integration with third-party security tools** for enhanced visibility.

IBM QRadar's AI capabilities **help organizations prioritize threats efficiently,** reducing investigation times and **enhancing incident response capabilities.**

Splunk Enterprise Security

Splunk Enterprise Security (ES) is a **cloud-native SIEM** that uses AI for **advanced threat analytics and real-time monitoring**. Key features include:

- **AI-powered behavioral analytics** to detect insider threats and compromised accounts.
- **Security automation and orchestration** to respond to incidents with minimal human intervention.
- **Machine learning-driven log analysis** to identify potential security vulnerabilities.

Splunk ES integrates with **various cloud services and on-premises security tools**, making it a **versatile solution for modern security operations centers (SOCs).**

Microsoft Sentinel

Microsoft Sentinel is a **cloud-native SIEM and security orchestration, automation, and response (SOAR) platform** that provides AI-driven security insights. Key capabilities include:

- **AI-powered incident correlation** to reduce false positives and improve response times.
- **Automated threat investigation and remediation** using Microsoft's security intelligence.
- **Deep integration with Azure and Microsoft 365 security services** for seamless protection.

Microsoft Sentinel is **highly scalable and designed for cloud-native security operations,** making it an ideal choice for enterprises operating in **hybrid and multi-cloud environments.**

AI-Driven Data Protection and Encryption in Cloud Environments

With the increasing adoption of cloud computing, **data security has become a top priority for businesses handling sensitive information.** AI-driven data protection mechanisms enhance traditional security approaches by **automating encryption, detecting anomalies, and preventing unauthorized data access.** AI-powered **encryption and data loss prevention (DLP) solutions** ensure that organizations can **safeguard their cloud-stored information while maintaining compliance** with industry regulations like **GDPR, HIPAA, and CCPA.**

1. AI-Enhanced Data Encryption

Encryption is a fundamental aspect of cloud security, ensuring that **data remains unreadable to unauthorized users**. However, **traditional encryption methods require manual key management and periodic updates**, which can be complex and prone to misconfigurations. AI improves encryption security by **automating key management, generating advanced encryption algorithms, and implementing dynamic data masking techniques**.

Automated Key Management

AI streamlines encryption key management by **automating key rotation, lifecycle monitoring, and revocation**. Traditional key management processes **require manual intervention**, increasing the risk of human error. AI-based key management solutions:

- Ensure **timely and secure key rotations** to minimize vulnerabilities.
- Prevent **unauthorized key access** by monitoring usage patterns and enforcing access controls.
- Enhance compliance with **industry standards** by enforcing encryption policies in cloud environments.

AI-Based Encryption Algorithms

AI aids in developing and optimizing **advanced encryption algorithms** to secure sensitive data. By analyzing **existing encryption standards and security threats**, AI-driven systems:

- **Generate stronger cryptographic algorithms** resistant to quantum computing threats.
- Continuously test encryption models against **real-world cyberattacks** to improve resilience.

- Recommend the most **efficient encryption techniques** based on the sensitivity of the data.

For example, AI-powered **homomorphic encryption** allows **data to be processed while still encrypted**, reducing the risk of exposure during computations in cloud environments.

Dynamic Data Masking

AI automates **dynamic data masking (DDM)** to protect sensitive information while allowing controlled access for authorized users. This is particularly useful in **multi-tenant cloud environments** where different levels of access need to be enforced. AI-driven DDM solutions:

- **Identify and classify sensitive data** (e.g., personally identifiable information, financial records).
- Apply **real-time masking techniques** to prevent unauthorized users from viewing confidential information.
- **Adaptively adjust masking policies** based on user behavior and contextual access patterns.

For example, AI can dynamically **redact credit card details** when accessed by customer service agents but **display full information** to authorized financial personnel.

2. AI for Data Loss Prevention (DLP)

AI-driven **Data Loss Prevention (DLP) solutions** protect sensitive data from accidental exposure or malicious exfiltration. AI enhances DLP systems by **automatically classifying data, detecting insider threats, and integrating with Cloud Access Security Brokers (CASB) to enforce security policies** across cloud environments.

Content-Aware DLP

Traditional DLP solutions rely on predefined rules to **identify and block sensitive data transmissions**, but these methods often result in **false positives and inefficiencies**. AI-powered content-aware DLP solutions:

- Use **Natural Language Processing (NLP) and machine learning** to **classify sensitive information** dynamically.
- Scan **emails, cloud storage, and collaboration platforms** for **unauthorized data sharing**.
- Adapt to **new compliance regulations and industry standards** by updating policies automatically.

For example, AI-driven DLP can **detect and prevent an employee from sending customer data via personal email** or **uploading confidential files to unauthorized cloud storage**.

AI-Based Insider Threat Detection

AI enhances **insider threat detection** by continuously analyzing user behavior and identifying **anomalous activities that may indicate data exfiltration**. AI-powered insider threat detection:

- Monitors **login patterns, file access history, and data downloads** for suspicious deviations.
- Uses **User and Entity Behavior Analytics (UEBA)** to detect **privilege abuse and data leaks**.
- Automatically generates **risk scores** for users based on their activity patterns and alerts security teams in case of anomalies.

For instance, if an employee **who has never accessed critical databases suddenly downloads large amounts of data**, AI-powered DLP will flag this as a potential **data exfiltration attempt**.

AI-Driven Cloud Access Security Brokers (CASB)

Cloud Access Security Brokers (CASB) **protect data across SaaS, IaaS, and PaaS environments** by enforcing security policies. AI-powered CASB solutions:

- Monitor **cloud application usage** to prevent **unauthorized data transfers**.
- Identify **shadow IT** (unauthorized applications) that pose security risks.
- Apply **adaptive access controls**, restricting or blocking access based on real-time risk assessments.

For example, if AI detects that an employee is attempting to **upload confidential files to an unapproved cloud service**, the CASB solution can **automatically block the upload and alert security teams**.

Compliance Challenges and AI-Based Solutions in Cloud Security

As organizations increasingly adopt cloud computing, **ensuring regulatory compliance** becomes a significant challenge. The dynamic nature of cloud environments, evolving regulations, and complex multi-cloud architectures create compliance risks that require **continuous monitoring and enforcement**. Traditional compliance management methods often struggle to keep up with these challenges, making **AI-driven solutions essential** for maintaining compliance efficiently.

1. Compliance Challenges in Cloud Security

Cloud environments **introduce complexities** in maintaining regulatory compliance due to factors such as **shared responsibility models, diverse cloud architectures, and constantly changing regulations**. Organizations must **navigate multiple compliance frameworks**, such as **GDPR, HIPAA, CCPA, ISO 27001, and SOC 2**, while ensuring data protection across **geographically distributed cloud infrastructures**.

Dynamic and Multi-Cloud Architectures

Modern enterprises often use a combination of **public, private, and hybrid cloud environments**, as well as multiple cloud service providers like **AWS, Azure, and Google Cloud**. This multi-cloud strategy **improves flexibility and scalability** but complicates compliance management due to:

- **Diverse security policies** across different cloud platforms.
- **Inconsistent access controls** and authentication mechanisms.
- **Lack of visibility** into cloud workloads and data movement.

For example, an organization using AWS for storage and Azure for compute services must ensure that **security policies, data encryption, and access controls align across both platforms**, which can be difficult to manage manually.

Evolving Regulatory Requirements

Regulatory compliance is **not static**—laws and industry standards are frequently updated to address **emerging cybersecurity threats and data privacy concerns**. Organizations must:

- **Monitor changes in regulations** to ensure continuous compliance.
- **Update security policies and procedures** based on new legal requirements.
- **Demonstrate compliance** through regular audits and reporting.

For instance, **GDPR mandates strict data protection measures**, requiring organizations to quickly **adapt security controls** whenever new rulings or amendments are introduced. Failure to comply can result in **hefty fines and reputational damage**.

Data Residency and Sovereignty

Cloud providers store and process data across **multiple geographic regions**, which poses challenges related to **data residency, sovereignty, and cross-border data transfers**. Compliance risks arise when:

- **Sensitive data is stored in regions with weak privacy laws.**
- **Different jurisdictions have conflicting data protection requirements.**
- **Organizations lack control over where their data is physically located.**

For example, **European data protection laws restrict the transfer of personal data outside the EU**, making it **challenging for multinational companies** to store customer data in global cloud environments while maintaining compliance.

2. AI-Based Compliance Solutions

AI-driven compliance solutions **enhance security governance, automate policy enforcement, and streamline regulatory adherence** in cloud environments. By leveraging **machine learning, natural language processing, and predictive analytics**, AI ensures that organizations can **proactively manage compliance risks** without manual intervention.

Automated Compliance Audits

AI automates compliance assessments by **continuously scanning cloud environments** for violations. This helps organizations:

- **Identify misconfigurations in real-time,** reducing security gaps.
- **Generate compliance reports automatically,** simplifying audit processes.
- **Detect policy deviations** across cloud workloads, applications, and services.

For instance, AI-powered tools like **AWS Config and Microsoft Purview** monitor cloud infrastructure to ensure adherence to **security best practices and compliance frameworks** such as **NIST, ISO 27001, and PCI DSS.**

AI-Driven Policy Enforcement

Enforcing security policies across **multi-cloud environments** is a significant challenge. AI improves policy enforcement by:

- **Automatically applying security controls** based on compliance requirements.
- **Enforcing least-privilege access policies** to prevent unauthorized data exposure.
- **Detecting unauthorized changes** to cloud configurations and rolling them back.

For example, **Google Cloud Security Command Center** uses AI to detect **non-compliant configurations** and automatically applies corrective actions, **ensuring continuous compliance** without manual intervention.

Regulatory Change Adaptation

Keeping up with evolving regulations is a complex task. AI helps organizations **adapt to new compliance mandates** by:

- **Monitoring regulatory changes across different jurisdictions.**
- **Providing recommendations on necessary security adjustments.**
- **Automatically updating compliance frameworks** to reflect the latest legal requirements.

For instance, AI-driven compliance management platforms like **IBM OpenPages and ServiceNow GRC** analyze **regulatory updates** and provide **actionable insights** to help organizations **maintain compliance with minimal effort.**

Summary

AI is revolutionizing cloud security by enabling real-time threat detection, automated incident response, and enhanced compliance management. AI-powered threat detection systems leverage behavioral analytics to identify anomalies, while AI-driven SIEM solutions provide real-time security insights. AI also strengthens data protection through intelligent encryption and data loss prevention techniques. Additionally, AI-based compliance solutions simplify regulatory adherence by automating audits and policy enforcement. As cyber threats continue to evolve, AI will play an increasingly vital role in safeguarding cloud environments and ensuring regulatory compliance.

Chapter 7: AI in Cloud Automation and DevOps

Introduction

As cloud environments become increasingly complex, traditional DevOps practices struggle to keep up with the demands of scalability, efficiency, and continuous delivery. Artificial Intelligence (AI) has become a game-changer in cloud automation and DevOps, enabling intelligent resource optimization, automated deployments, and real-time performance monitoring. This chapter explores AI-driven cloud resource optimization, AI in CI/CD pipelines, AIOps for cloud performance monitoring, and AI's role in Kubernetes and containerized environments.

AI for Cloud Resource Optimization and Auto-Scaling

Managing cloud resources efficiently is **critical for maintaining performance, minimizing costs, and ensuring seamless scalability**. Traditional cloud resource management relies on **manual provisioning and reactive scaling**, which often leads to **over-provisioning (wasting resources) or under-provisioning (causing performance issues)**. AI-driven optimization transforms cloud resource allocation by using **machine learning algorithms and predictive analytics** to automate scaling, **optimize workloads, and reduce operational costs**.

1. AI-Driven Cloud Resource Optimization

Cloud environments host **diverse workloads**, each with fluctuating demands. AI enhances cloud resource management by **dynamically** allocating computing power based on real-time and historical data patterns, ensuring that cloud infrastructure remains cost-effective, energy-efficient, and highly available.

Predictive Auto-Scaling

Traditional auto-scaling mechanisms respond to spikes reactively, often causing delays in provisioning additional resources when demand surges. AI-powered predictive auto-scaling takes a proactive approach by:

- Analyzing historical usage trends to anticipate future workloads.
- Allocating resources before demand spikes occur, preventing performance degradation.
- Reducing downtime and latency by ensuring applications always have the right resources.

For instance, AWS Auto Scaling and Google Kubernetes Engine (GKE) Autopilot leverage AI-based predictions to dynamically allocate compute, storage, and networking resources, ensuring uninterrupted application performance during peak traffic periods.

Intelligent Load Balancing

Cloud applications serve millions of users globally, leading to unpredictable traffic fluctuations. AI-driven load balancing optimizes traffic distribution by:

- Analyzing real-time traffic loads to distribute requests efficiently.
- Identifying and mitigating performance bottlenecks in cloud environments.
- Redirecting workloads to underutilized servers to balance computational efficiency.

For example, **Microsoft Azure Load Balancer** and **Google Cloud Load Balancing** use **AI-based traffic analytics** to intelligently route user requests across multiple servers, ensuring low latency and high availability.

Energy-Efficient Computing

Data centers consume vast amounts of energy, leading to **high operational costs and increased carbon footprints**. AI-driven **energy optimization** helps cloud providers and enterprises:

- **Adjust power consumption dynamically** based on workload intensity.
- **Optimize cooling mechanisms** by analyzing real-time temperature and power usage.
- **Predict and reduce unnecessary idle resource usage**, lowering overall electricity costs.

For instance, **Google's AI-powered data centers** have reduced cooling costs by **40%** through **real-time energy efficiency optimizations**, demonstrating how AI can make cloud computing more sustainable.

2. AI-Powered Cost Optimization

Cloud services follow a **pay-as-you-go pricing model**, which, if not optimized, can lead to **uncontrolled spending**. Organizations often struggle with **unused resources, inefficient provisioning, and unpredictable billing spikes**. AI-driven solutions **identify cost-saving opportunities, optimize resource allocation, and prevent budget overruns**.

Automated Cost Monitoring

Manually tracking cloud expenses across multiple services is **time-consuming and error-prone**. AI simplifies cost monitoring by:

- **Analyzing billing data in real-time** to track spending patterns.
- **Detecting unused or underutilized resources** and recommending deallocation.
- **Identifying cost anomalies** and notifying teams before excessive charges occur.

For instance, **AWS Cost Anomaly Detection** and **Google Cloud Cost Management** use **AI-powered analytics** to **detect unexpected billing increases and alert administrators** before costs spiral out of control.

Rightsizing Recommendations

Many cloud workloads operate on **over-provisioned resources,** leading to unnecessary expenses. AI-driven **rightsizing** helps optimize resource allocation by:

- **Analyzing workload performance metrics** to determine the optimal instance types.
- **Suggesting smaller or more cost-effective instances** without compromising performance.
- **Automatically scaling down resources** when peak demand subsides.

For example, **AWS Compute Optimizer** and **Azure Advisor** use **AI-driven insights** to **recommend appropriate VM sizes and storage configurations,** allowing organizations to optimize cloud costs without affecting application performance.

Real-Time Anomaly Detection

Unexpected cost spikes can occur due to **misconfigurations, unintentional provisioning, or security breaches**. AI-powered anomaly detection prevents budget overruns by:

- **Identifying unusual spending patterns** across cloud resources.
- **Detecting unauthorized deployments or excessive resource usage.**
- **Sending real-time alerts to administrators** before budgets are exceeded.

For example, **Google Cloud Recommender** and **AWS Budgets** use **AI-powered anomaly detection** to identify **unexpected cost variations,** helping organizations maintain **financial control over their cloud infrastructure.**

AI in Cloud-Based CI/CD Pipelines

The integration of **Artificial Intelligence (AI) in Continuous Integration (CI) and Continuous Deployment (CD) pipelines** has transformed software development by **automating error detection, optimizing deployment processes, and ensuring higher code quality.** Traditional CI/CD workflows rely on **manual testing, scripted automation, and human intervention,** which often result in **delayed releases, undetected vulnerabilities, and inefficient resource utilization.** AI-driven enhancements introduce **intelligent automation, predictive analytics, and real-time monitoring,** making CI/CD pipelines more **resilient, adaptive, and efficient.**

1. Enhancing Continuous Integration (CI) with AI

Continuous Integration (CI) focuses on **automating code integration, testing, and validation** to ensure that new changes do not introduce bugs or performance issues. AI-driven CI solutions **streamline testing, detect security vulnerabilities, and optimize build performance,** significantly reducing the chances of failed deployments.

AI-Based Code Analysis

AI-powered tools analyze source code to **identify vulnerabilities, security risks, and performance inefficiencies** before deployment. These tools use **machine learning (ML) models** to detect:

- **Code smells and anti-patterns** that may impact maintainability.
- **Potential security vulnerabilities**, such as SQL injections or buffer overflows.
- **Performance bottlenecks** in application logic or database queries.

Tools like **SonarQube, DeepCode, and Codacy** leverage **AI-based static code analysis** to automatically detect **coding errors and security flaws**, ensuring that only high-quality code progresses through the CI pipeline.

Automated Testing with AI

Traditional testing methods often rely on **predefined test scripts**, which can be **time-consuming to create and maintain**. AI-driven testing frameworks:

- **Automatically generate optimal test cases** by analyzing previous test runs and predicting failure points.
- **Reduce test execution time** by prioritizing test cases based on potential impact.
- **Improve test coverage** by dynamically adapting to code changes.

AI-powered tools like **Testim, Functionize, and Applitools** use **machine learning models to detect UI changes, performance degradations, and functional errors**, ensuring robust testing without manual intervention.

Fault Prediction and Prevention

AI enhances CI pipelines by analyzing **historical build failures** and predicting potential issues before they occur. AI-based fault prediction:

- **Identifies recurring patterns** in failed builds.
- **Flags risky code commits** based on developer coding history and past errors.
- **Suggests corrective actions** to prevent build failures before they happen.

For example, **GitHub Copilot** and **Google's AI-powered Cloud Build** use AI-driven insights to recommend **code improvements and bug fixes**, reducing the likelihood of defects in production.

2. AI-Driven Continuous Deployment (CD)

Continuous Deployment (CD) automates the **release and deployment** of applications to production environments. AI enhances CD by **minimizing downtime, optimizing release schedules, and enabling intelligent rollback mechanisms** to prevent service disruptions.

Intelligent Rollback Mechanisms

Traditional rollback mechanisms require **manual intervention or pre-scripted conditions** to revert failed deployments. AI-driven rollback systems:

- **Predict potential deployment failures** by analyzing past incidents.
- **Monitor key performance indicators (KPIs)** in real-time to detect anomalies.
- **Trigger automatic rollback actions** before users experience downtime.

For instance, **AWS CodeDeploy and Kubernetes Rollbacks** leverage AI-based **health monitoring** to roll back deployments when they detect performance degradation or security risks.

Automated Release Orchestration

AI optimizes deployment schedules by analyzing:

- **Traffic patterns and user behavior** to determine the best release time.
- **Infrastructure availability** to avoid overloading cloud resources.
- **Potential risks associated with concurrent deployments** in multi-cloud environments.

AI-based deployment management tools like **Google Cloud Deploy, Harness, and Spinnaker** automate release workflows, ensuring that **new features are rolled out efficiently without service interruptions**.

Canary and Blue-Green Deployments

To ensure **seamless deployments with minimal risk**, AI enhances **progressive rollout strategies** like:

- **Canary Deployments**: AI monitors a small percentage of live users exposed to a new release, detecting issues before a full rollout.
- **Blue-Green Deployments**: AI helps switch between old (Blue) and new (Green) environments based on real-time performance insights.

AI-powered **observability platforms** like **Datadog, New Relic, and Dynatrace** analyze **real-time user experience metrics**, allowing teams to make data-driven decisions on **when to fully release or rollback** new versions.

AI-Driven IT Operations (AIOps) for Cloud Performance Monitoring

Modern IT environments are becoming **increasingly complex**, with organizations managing **multi-cloud infrastructures, hybrid environments, and distributed applications**. Traditional IT operations struggle to keep up with the sheer volume of **logs, alerts, and performance data** generated across cloud ecosystems. This is where **Artificial Intelligence for IT Operations (AIOps)** comes in.

AIOps leverages **machine learning, big data analytics, and automation** to **streamline IT operations, reduce downtime, and enhance system performance**. By integrating AI into IT operations, organizations can achieve **predictive maintenance, intelligent incident resolution, and real-time monitoring**, ultimately ensuring **higher system availability and efficiency**.

1. What is AIOps?

AIOps applies **AI and data analytics** to automate and optimize IT operations. Traditional monitoring tools rely on **threshold-based alerts** and **manual interventions**, leading to **delayed incident response** and **prolonged outages**. AIOps overcomes these limitations by:

Predictive Maintenance

AIOps predicts **hardware failures, software crashes, and system anomalies** before they cause downtime. By analyzing historical data and identifying early warning signs, AI-driven systems:

- **Detect disk failures, memory leaks, and CPU spikes** before they impact performance.
- **Predict potential system crashes** based on past patterns and real-time telemetry data.

- **Optimize resource allocation** by recommending proactive adjustments to cloud infrastructure.

For instance, AI-powered platforms like **Google Cloud Operations Suite (formerly Stackdriver)** use predictive analytics to **anticipate outages and suggest preventive actions** before they occur.

Automated Incident Resolution

One of the biggest advantages of AIOps is its ability to **resolve IT incidents autonomously.** AI-driven chatbots and virtual assistants:

- **Analyze and categorize IT support tickets** based on historical resolution data.
- **Provide automated troubleshooting steps** for common IT issues.
- **Trigger automated workflows** to resolve incidents without human intervention.

For example, **ServiceNow's AI-driven Virtual Agent** can **handle repetitive IT support tasks**, such as password resets and system diagnostics, freeing up IT teams to focus on more complex problems.

Real-Time Performance Monitoring

AI continuously monitors **cloud infrastructure, applications, and network traffic**, ensuring **optimal performance** at all times. AIOps solutions analyze metrics such as:

- **CPU and memory utilization** across cloud instances.
- **Application response times and user experience metrics.**
- **Network latency and traffic patterns** to detect anomalies.

Unlike traditional monitoring tools that **generate static alerts**, AI-driven monitoring **correlates data from multiple sources**, identifying **root causes faster and reducing alert fatigue.**

For instance, **AWS CloudWatch and Microsoft Azure Monitor** integrate AI-powered anomaly detection to **identify performance degradation before it impacts end users.**

2. Leading AIOps Tools

AIOps platforms have gained **significant traction** in cloud performance monitoring, with major vendors offering AI-powered solutions for **automated IT operations management.** Some of the leading AIOps tools include:

IBM Watson AIOps

IBM Watson AIOps is an AI-driven IT operations platform that **automates incident detection, diagnosis, and resolution.** It leverages:

- **Natural Language Processing (NLP)** to analyze unstructured IT logs and identify patterns.
- **Machine learning models** to predict system failures and recommend corrective actions.
- **Automated anomaly detection** to reduce false alerts and improve operational efficiency.

IBM Watson AIOps helps organizations **minimize downtime and optimize cloud performance** by intelligently correlating IT data across hybrid cloud environments.

Dynatrace

Dynatrace provides an **AI-powered observability platform** for **full-stack monitoring** across cloud, containers, and microservices architectures. Key features include:

- **Davis AI Engine**: A built-in AI model that **automatically detects performance anomalies** and pinpoints root causes.
- **Automatic dependency mapping** to visualize relationships between applications and infrastructure components.
- **Self-healing capabilities** that enable cloud resources to recover automatically from failures.

With its **real-time AI-driven insights**, Dynatrace helps DevOps and IT teams **proactively manage cloud performance and user experience**.

Splunk IT Service Intelligence (ITSI)

Splunk ITSI is an **AI-powered IT operations platform** designed for **event correlation, anomaly detection, and predictive analytics**. It enables organizations to:

- **Analyze massive volumes of IT data** to identify trends and patterns.
- **Use AI-driven event correlation** to reduce noise from alerts and focus on critical issues.
- **Predict system failures and security incidents** before they escalate.

By integrating **Splunk ITSI** into cloud environments, IT teams can **gain real-time visibility into cloud operations and proactively address performance bottlenecks**.

The Role of AI in Kubernetes and Containerized Environments

Kubernetes has become the **de facto standard** for container orchestration, enabling organizations to manage **large-scale containerized applications** efficiently. However, as deployments grow in complexity, managing **scalability, security, resource optimization, and fault tolerance** becomes increasingly challenging. **Artificial Intelligence (AI) is transforming Kubernetes operations** by automating **resource allocation, security monitoring, and anomaly detection**, reducing manual intervention and improving operational efficiency.

By integrating AI into **Kubernetes-based environments**, organizations can achieve **self-healing clusters, intelligent workload distribution, and proactive security enforcement**, ensuring **high availability, cost optimization, and robust protection** for cloud-native applications.

1. AI-Enhanced Kubernetes Management

Managing Kubernetes clusters manually can be time-consuming and inefficient, especially in **large-scale, multi-cloud, or hybrid environments**. AI simplifies Kubernetes operations by automating critical tasks such as **scaling, monitoring, and security enforcement**, leading to **more resilient and cost-effective containerized applications**.

Self-Healing Kubernetes Clusters

Kubernetes inherently offers self-healing capabilities, but AI **enhances this feature by predicting failures and automating resolutions**. AI-driven Kubernetes management tools:

- **Continuously monitor container health** and restart failed containers automatically.

- **Analyze historical failure patterns** to predict and prevent similar issues.
- **Optimize auto-scaling decisions** to maintain application performance and stability.

For example, **Google Kubernetes Engine (GKE) Autopilot** leverages **machine learning models** to automatically optimize cluster configurations, ensuring **maximum uptime with minimal manual intervention.**

Automated Workload Placement

AI-driven workload placement ensures **optimal resource utilization** by dynamically scheduling workloads based on **real-time cluster conditions.** AI algorithms consider factors such as:

- **CPU and memory availability** across nodes.
- **Network traffic patterns and latency requirements.**
- **Application-specific dependencies** and resource demands.

By intelligently distributing workloads, AI **minimizes performance bottlenecks, reduces congestion, and improves efficiency** in Kubernetes environments.

For instance, **Kubernetes AI-driven schedulers** like **KubeFlow and Karmada** use deep learning to **predict resource demand and assign workloads to the most suitable nodes,** enhancing overall cluster performance.

Optimized Kubernetes Cost Management

AI helps **optimize Kubernetes resource usage and reduce cloud costs** by identifying **underutilized resources and unnecessary allocations.** AI-powered cost management tools:

- **Analyze cloud billing data** and recommend cost-saving measures.
- **Automatically scale down unused or idle containers**, reducing wasted compute power.
- **Suggest optimal instance types** based on real-time workload demand.

For example, **Kubecost** is an AI-driven tool that provides **real-time cost monitoring, waste detection, and budget forecasts**, allowing organizations to **maximize cost efficiency in Kubernetes clusters**.

2. AI-Driven Container Security

Security is a major concern in **containerized environments**, as containers introduce new attack vectors, including **image vulnerabilities, misconfigurations, and runtime threats**. AI strengthens security by **automating threat detection, vulnerability scanning, and policy enforcement**, reducing the risk of breaches and unauthorized access.

Threat Detection and Response

AI enhances container security by continuously **monitoring container behavior** and detecting **anomalies in real-time**. AI-powered security platforms:

- **Analyze container network traffic and process activity** to detect unusual patterns.
- **Identify insider threats and external attacks** through behavioral analysis.
- **Automatically block suspicious activities and trigger response mechanisms**.

For example, **Palo Alto Networks Prisma Cloud** and **Aqua Security** leverage AI-powered anomaly detection to **identify and mitigate** security threats in Kubernetes environments, preventing unauthorized access and data breaches.

Automated Vulnerability Scanning

AI-driven vulnerability scanners ensure **container images are free from security flaws before deployment**. These scanners:

- **Continuously check container registries for known vulnerabilities** (CVE detection).
- **Analyze software dependencies and package versions** for outdated components.
- **Provide automated remediation suggestions** to mitigate security risks.

Popular AI-based vulnerability scanning tools like **Snyk, Clair, and Trivy** help organizations **secure their containerized applications by identifying and fixing vulnerabilities before they reach production**.

AI-Based Policy Enforcement

Maintaining **consistent security policies across multiple Kubernetes clusters** can be challenging. AI simplifies compliance and security enforcement by:

- **Automatically applying predefined security policies** across all containers.
- **Detecting policy violations and suggesting corrective actions**.
- **Ensuring regulatory compliance** with frameworks like **GDPR, PCI-DSS, and HIPAA**.

For example, **Kyverno and Open Policy Agent (OPA)** use **AI-enhanced policy enforcement** to ensure Kubernetes configurations adhere to security best practices, reducing **misconfigurations and compliance risks**.

Summary

AI is revolutionizing cloud automation and DevOps by optimizing resource allocation, enhancing CI/CD pipelines, and automating IT operations. AI-powered solutions enable predictive scaling, intelligent workload distribution, and cost optimization in cloud environments. AIOps further enhances cloud performance monitoring, enabling real-time anomaly detection and automated incident resolution. Additionally, AI plays a crucial role in managing Kubernetes and containerized workloads by improving security, efficiency, and self-healing capabilities. As cloud complexity grows, AI-driven automation will be instrumental in driving efficiency, security, and reliability in cloud computing and DevOps practices.

Part 3: Industry Use Cases and Real-World Applications

Chapter 8: AI and Cloud in Business Transformation

Introduction

The fusion of Artificial Intelligence (AI) and cloud computing is transforming business operations across industries. Companies leverage AI-driven insights, automation, and predictive analytics to improve decision-making, enhance customer experiences, and optimize financial and retail operations. This chapter explores AI-driven business intelligence, AI-powered customer experience in cloud services, AI for financial forecasting and fraud detection, and AI-enhanced cloud solutions for retail and e-commerce.

AI-Driven Business Intelligence and Cloud Analytics

Artificial Intelligence (AI) is transforming **Business Intelligence (BI) and cloud analytics** by enabling businesses to **analyze vast amounts of data, recognize patterns, and generate insights in real-time**. AI-powered BI solutions **enhance decision-making, automate data processing, and provide predictive analytics** to help organizations stay ahead in competitive markets. By leveraging **AI-driven cloud analytics tools**, businesses can **extract meaningful insights, reduce operational costs, and improve efficiency.**

As companies continue to **generate and store massive amounts of data in the cloud**, AI-powered analytics solutions are becoming **indispensable**. These technologies **enhance accuracy, automate reporting, and provide deeper insights into market trends, customer behavior, and operational performance.** With AI-integrated BI, organizations can **move beyond traditional data analysis methods** and embrace a more intelligent, data-driven decision-making approach.

1. The Role of AI in Business Intelligence (BI)

AI plays a crucial role in **enhancing Business Intelligence (BI) by** enabling **real-time data processing, pattern recognition, and automated reporting**. These AI-driven capabilities help businesses **improve forecasting, automate workflows, and make strategic decisions faster and more accurately.**

Predictive Analytics for Proactive Decision-Making

One of the most significant benefits of AI in BI is **predictive analytics,** which uses **machine learning (ML) models to analyze historical data and predict future trends.** AI-driven predictive analytics allows businesses to:

- **Forecast customer demand and market trends** based on past behaviors.
- **Identify potential risks** and mitigate them before they impact operations.
- **Optimize supply chain and inventory management,** ensuring better resource allocation.

For example, **retailers use AI-powered predictive analytics to determine which products will be in high demand** during certain seasons, allowing them to **optimize inventory and avoid stock shortages or overstocking.** Similarly, **financial institutions leverage AI-driven models to detect potential fraud patterns,** ensuring **proactive security measures.**

Automated Data Processing for Increased Efficiency

Traditionally, data processing requires **significant manual effort**, including **data cleansing, integration, and visualization**. AI eliminates these inefficiencies by **automating repetitive tasks**, allowing businesses to:

- **Clean and preprocess raw data**, reducing inconsistencies and errors.
- **Integrate data from multiple sources**, such as databases, IoT devices, and cloud storage.
- **Generate visual reports and dashboards** with minimal human intervention.

For instance, **AI-powered ETL (Extract, Transform, Load) tools automate data transformation processes**, enabling businesses to **focus on insights rather than data preparation**. This significantly **reduces workload, minimizes human errors, and speeds up analysis**.

Enhanced Decision-Making with AI-Powered Insights

AI-powered BI tools help organizations **make smarter business decisions** by analyzing vast datasets and identifying **patterns, correlations, and anomalies** that may be missed by human analysts. These tools:

- **Provide real-time insights** to improve operational efficiency.
- **Offer data-driven recommendations** based on AI-generated models.
- **Improve strategic planning** by identifying business growth opportunities.

For example, **AI-powered BI dashboards in industries like healthcare and finance help executives monitor key performance** indicators (KPIs) in real-time, allowing them to make **informed decisions quickly and effectively.**

2. Cloud-Based AI Analytics Tools

With the increasing adoption of **cloud computing**, many cloud service providers offer **AI-driven analytics solutions** to help businesses **leverage data more efficiently.** These tools **integrate AI and machine learning capabilities** to enhance **data processing, visualization, and reporting.** Some of the leading cloud-based AI analytics tools include:

Google Cloud BigQuery

Google Cloud BigQuery is a **serverless, highly scalable data warehouse** that enables businesses to run **fast SQL queries on large datasets.** With built-in AI and machine learning (ML) capabilities, BigQuery helps organizations:

- **Analyze massive datasets in real-time** without requiring complex infrastructure.
- **Integrate AI-powered models** directly within the database.
- **Improve query performance and optimize cost efficiency** with automatic scaling.

BigQuery's **ML features** allow businesses to **train machine learning models using structured data** without moving data outside the platform, ensuring **security and efficiency.**

AWS QuickSight

Amazon QuickSight is an **AI-powered BI service** that enables organizations to create **interactive dashboards and visual reports.** It offers:

- **Built-in machine learning insights** to detect trends and anomalies.
- **Automated data discovery and visualization** for faster insights.
- **Scalable, serverless BI infrastructure** that adapts to business needs.

QuickSight's **ML-powered anomaly detection** automatically identifies **unexpected changes in data**, helping businesses **proactively address operational challenges.** This tool is widely used by enterprises to **monitor sales trends, financial performance, and customer engagement metrics.**

Microsoft Azure Synapse Analytics

Azure Synapse Analytics is a **cloud-based analytics service** that integrates **big data and AI-driven insights** for advanced business intelligence. It allows businesses to:

- **Perform real-time analytics on massive datasets.**
- **Integrate AI and ML models directly within SQL queries.**
- **Utilize predictive analytics and automated data processing** for strategic decision-making.

Azure Synapse's AI-powered features **help businesses identify customer behavior patterns, optimize marketing strategies, and detect operational inefficiencies.** By combining **big data processing and AI,** organizations can **extract deeper insights and drive data-driven innovation.**

AI-Powered Customer Experience in Cloud Services

Artificial Intelligence (AI) is **revolutionizing customer experience (CX) in cloud services** by **enhancing communication, personalizing interactions, and automating service delivery.** With

AI-powered tools, businesses can provide **real-time assistance, understand customer sentiments, and optimize engagement strategies.** The integration of AI in cloud-based customer experience solutions allows organizations to **scale support operations, improve customer satisfaction, and drive higher retention rates.**

Cloud providers are leveraging AI-driven technologies like **chatbots, sentiment analysis, and voice/image recognition** to create **seamless and intuitive customer interactions.** These advancements **reduce response times, improve accuracy in support responses, and enable hyper-personalized services** across various industries, including **e-commerce, banking, and healthcare.**

1. AI Chatbots and Virtual Assistants

AI-driven **chatbots and virtual assistants** are transforming **customer support and engagement** by offering **instant, 24/7 assistance, personalized interactions, and automated issue resolution.**

24/7 Customer Assistance

AI chatbots operate **round-the-clock,** providing **instant responses to customer queries without human intervention.** This ensures:

- **Reduced wait times** and improved **customer satisfaction.**
- **Consistent service quality,** regardless of time zones.
- **Scalability,** allowing businesses to handle large volumes of inquiries efficiently.

For instance, **cloud-based AI chatbots like Google Dialogflow, IBM Watson Assistant, and Amazon Lex** help enterprises automate **support requests, FAQs, and service bookings** without requiring **human customer agents.**

Personalized Interactions

AI analyzes **customer data, purchase history, and browsing behavior** to **deliver personalized responses and recommendations**. By leveraging **machine learning (ML) algorithms**, chatbots can:

- **Identify returning customers** and tailor conversations based on past interactions.
- **Provide product or service recommendations** based on user preferences.
- **Offer dynamic responses** that adapt to evolving customer needs.

For example, **e-commerce platforms like Amazon and Shopify** use AI-driven virtual assistants to **offer tailored product recommendations based on browsing history**.

Automated Problem Resolution

AI-powered bots can **resolve common customer issues autonomously**, reducing dependency on human agents. AI enables:

- **Instant troubleshooting for technical issues** by guiding users through solutions.
- **Automated refunds, cancellations, or policy-related inquiries** through natural language processing (NLP).
- **Seamless escalation to human agents when necessary**, ensuring complex queries are handled efficiently.

For example, **banking institutions use AI bots to automate account inquiries, transaction tracking, and fraud alerts**, significantly **reducing response times and enhancing security**.

2. Sentiment Analysis and Personalized Marketing

AI empowers businesses to **understand customer emotions and preferences**, allowing them to **tailor marketing strategies, improve customer engagement, and enhance brand loyalty.**

Sentiment Analysis for Customer Feedback

AI-driven **sentiment analysis tools** evaluate **customer reviews, social media mentions, and feedback** to measure customer sentiment in real-time. These tools:

- **Analyze text-based feedback** to determine whether sentiments are **positive, negative, or neutral.**
- **Detect emerging trends and common concerns**, allowing businesses to take **proactive action.**
- **Enhance brand reputation management** by identifying **customer pain points** and addressing them effectively.

For instance, **brands like Coca-Cola and Netflix use AI-driven sentiment analysis to monitor customer satisfaction and improve their marketing campaigns.**

AI-Driven Personalization for Targeted Marketing

AI enhances **customer engagement by tailoring product recommendations and marketing messages** based on **individual behavior patterns.** AI-driven personalization:

- **Optimizes email marketing campaigns**, sending messages based on customer activity.
- **Recommends relevant products** to users based on browsing and purchase history.
- **Predicts customer preferences**, allowing businesses to create **hyper-personalized shopping experiences.**

For example, **Spotify's AI-driven recommendation engine analyzes listening habits to create customized playlists, improving user engagement**. Similarly, **Amazon's AI suggests products based on past purchases, increasing conversion rates**.

3. AI-Enhanced Voice and Image Recognition

AI-powered **voice and image recognition technologies** are transforming **how customers interact with digital platforms**, making experiences **more intuitive and accessible**.

Voice Assistants for Enhanced Customer Interactions

AI-driven **voice recognition technology** enables **hands-free interactions** and enhances **voice-based search capabilities**. Businesses use voice AI to:

- **Enable voice-based product search** on e-commerce platforms.
- **Enhance call center operations** by transcribing and analyzing customer inquiries.
- **Improve accessibility for visually impaired users** by offering **voice-controlled navigation.**

Popular AI voice assistants like **Amazon Alexa, Google Assistant, and Apple Siri** use NLP and deep learning to **understand and respond to voice commands accurately**.

Image-Based Product Search and Visual Recognition

AI-powered **computer vision technology** allows customers to **search for products using images instead of text-based queries**. This feature:

- **Enhances e-commerce experiences** by enabling users to find similar products through image uploads.
- **Improves fraud detection in financial services** by analyzing document authenticity through AI-powered image verification.
- **Enables security enhancements**, such as **facial recognition authentication** for secure login processes.

For instance, **Google Lens allows users to take a photo of an item and search for similar products online**, streamlining the shopping experience. Similarly, **retail giants like Zara and ASOS use AI-powered visual search tools to improve product discovery**.

Cloud-Based AI for Financial Forecasting and Fraud Detection

The financial sector has always been data-driven, relying on **accurate forecasting, risk management, and fraud prevention** to ensure stability and growth. With the integration of **cloud-based AI technologies**, financial institutions can now process vast amounts of data in real-time, detect anomalies faster, and generate **more precise financial forecasts**. AI-powered solutions in finance enable businesses to **predict market trends, mitigate risks, ensure regulatory compliance, and protect against fraud**.

By leveraging cloud-based AI, companies can **automate complex financial processes**, reducing manual intervention and **enhancing operational efficiency**. AI-driven solutions also offer **greater scalability**, allowing financial firms to **adapt to fluctuating market conditions and regulatory changes seamlessly**. This transformation is not only improving decision-making but also reinforcing security and trust in financial transactions.

1. AI-Driven Financial Forecasting

Financial forecasting is critical for **business planning, investment decisions, and risk assessment.** AI has revolutionized this domain by enabling **predictive modeling, real-time data processing, and automated financial reporting.** Traditional financial forecasting methods relied heavily on **historical data and manual calculations,** making them prone to errors and inefficiencies. With AI, businesses can now **generate accurate forecasts faster and more efficiently.**

Predictive Modeling for Market Trends and Financial Planning

AI-driven predictive modeling leverages **machine learning (ML) algorithms** to analyze historical financial data and **identify patterns that help predict future revenues, expenses, and market risks.** These models can:

- **Forecast revenue growth and market fluctuations,** allowing businesses to make **data-driven investment decisions.**
- **Assess potential risks** in business operations, helping companies mitigate financial losses.
- **Optimize resource allocation** by predicting future demand and cost structures.

For instance, AI-powered **predictive models in investment banking analyze global economic indicators** to forecast stock market trends. Similarly, **retail businesses use AI to anticipate seasonal sales fluctuations,** ensuring **better inventory and financial planning.**

Real-Time Data Processing for Dynamic Forecasting

AI enhances financial forecasting by **processing large volumes of financial data in real-time.** This capability allows businesses to:

- **Adapt to changing market conditions instantly**, rather than relying on outdated reports.
- **Detect and respond to economic shifts proactively**, ensuring business continuity.
- **Improve decision-making with up-to-the-minute financial insights.**

For example, **AI-driven trading platforms use real-time data feeds to adjust stock portfolios** based on market trends. This enables investors to make **faster and more informed decisions**, minimizing financial risks.

Automated Reporting for Financial Insights

AI automates financial reporting by **analyzing data and generating comprehensive reports without manual intervention.** These reports:

- **Identify financial strengths and weaknesses** based on past performance.
- **Provide actionable insights for strategic business growth.**
- **Help executives and stakeholders make informed decisions** based on accurate financial data.

By automating reporting, **companies save time and reduce errors**, allowing financial analysts to focus on **high-level strategy and planning** rather than manual data processing.

2. AI-Powered Fraud Detection and Risk Management

Fraud prevention is a top priority for **banks, payment processors, and financial institutions.** AI-driven fraud detection systems **identify suspicious activities, monitor user behavior, and send real-time alerts** to prevent financial losses. By leveraging **machine learning algorithms and anomaly detection**, AI can **analyze massive** transaction datasets and flag potentially fraudulent activities in real-time.

Anomaly Detection for Identifying Fraudulent Transactions

AI-powered **anomaly detection algorithms** can identify unusual patterns in financial transactions, such as:

- **Uncharacteristic spending behaviors**, like sudden high-value transactions.
- **Multiple transactions from different locations within a short time frame.**
- **Unusual login attempts from unfamiliar devices or locations.**

For example, **AI in credit card fraud detection can instantly flag unauthorized purchases** by analyzing deviations from a user's spending habits. This enables banks to **block suspicious transactions before they lead to financial losses.**

Behavioral Analysis for Detecting Suspicious Activities

AI continuously **monitors user behavior** to detect **potential fraud or security breaches.** By analyzing:

- **Spending patterns and transaction history**, AI can identify **potential identity theft.**
- **Login attempts and access frequency**, AI can flag unauthorized account takeovers.
- **Time spent on financial portals**, AI can detect fraudulent interactions, such as **bot-driven cyberattacks.**

Behavioral analytics enable **financial institutions to take proactive measures**, such as **requesting additional authentication steps** if a transaction seems suspicious.

Real-Time Alerts for Immediate Action

AI systems **instantly notify banks, merchants, or users** when they detect fraudulent activities. These real-time alerts:

- **Reduce response time**, preventing unauthorized transactions.
- **Enhance security**, ensuring financial transactions remain safe.
- **Minimize financial damage**, allowing businesses to act swiftly.

For example, **banks using AI-powered fraud detection can automatically freeze an account if multiple suspicious transactions occur within minutes,** protecting the user from **further financial losses.**

3. AI-Based Regulatory Compliance in Financial Services

Financial institutions must adhere to **strict regulatory requirements** to ensure compliance with industry standards and government regulations. AI-powered compliance solutions help businesses:

- **Monitor financial transactions** for regulatory violations.
- **Automate compliance reporting and audit trails.**
- **Assess regulatory risks and suggest corrective actions.**

Automated Audit Trails for Compliance Tracking

AI **tracks and records all financial transactions**, ensuring that businesses comply with legal and regulatory requirements. Automated audit trails:

- **Reduce human errors in financial reporting.**
- **Ensure transparency and accountability.**
- **Make regulatory audits more efficient and streamlined.**

For example, **banks use AI to track money laundering activities** by monitoring large-scale financial transactions and reporting suspicious activities to authorities.

Regulatory Risk Assessment for Compliance Optimization

AI assesses **regulatory risks by analyzing financial data** and detecting compliance gaps. This allows businesses to:

- **Identify potential regulatory violations** before they occur.
- **Recommend actions to mitigate compliance risks.**
- **Ensure businesses stay updated with evolving regulations.**

For instance, **AI-powered compliance platforms in investment firms help ensure adherence to SEC (Securities and Exchange Commission) regulations**, reducing the risk of **legal penalties and financial losses.**

Intelligent Document Processing for Regulatory Reporting

AI automates document verification and regulatory reporting by:

- **Extracting relevant data from financial documents.**
- **Filling compliance forms automatically.**
- **Ensuring reports are error-free and submitted on time.**

By automating regulatory compliance processes, **financial institutions save time, reduce costs, and minimize regulatory risks.**

AI-Enhanced Cloud Solutions for Retail and E-Commerce

The retail and e-commerce industries have undergone a significant transformation with the integration of **AI-driven cloud solutions.** These advanced technologies enable businesses to **enhance operational** efficiency, **personalize customer experiences, and strengthen fraud prevention measures.** AI-powered tools can analyze vast amounts of data, **predict market trends, optimize inventory management, and improve customer engagement,** ultimately leading to **higher profitability and improved customer satisfaction.**

As competition in the retail and e-commerce space continues to grow, businesses must **leverage AI-driven solutions to stay ahead.** AI enables retailers to make **data-driven decisions, automate routine processes, and provide customers with a seamless shopping experience.** From **inventory optimization to fraud detection,** AI in cloud-based retail solutions is **reshaping the future of commerce.**

1. AI in Inventory and Supply Chain Management

Effective inventory and supply chain management are **critical for the success of retail and e-commerce businesses.** AI-driven solutions help businesses **optimize stock levels, streamline logistics, and reduce operational costs.** By leveraging **predictive analytics, automation, and real-time data processing,** AI ensures that businesses maintain **the right inventory levels while minimizing waste and shortages.**

Demand Forecasting for Optimized Inventory Planning

AI-powered demand forecasting analyzes **historical sales data, market trends, and consumer behavior** to predict future inventory needs accurately. This enables businesses to:

- **Anticipate demand fluctuations** and adjust stock levels accordingly.
- **Avoid overstocking or stockouts,** improving cost efficiency.
- **Enhance supplier coordination,** ensuring timely replenishment of products.

For example, **e-commerce platforms use AI to predict seasonal demand for popular items**, allowing retailers to stock up before peak shopping periods. Similarly, AI-driven demand forecasting helps grocery stores minimize food waste by ensuring that perishable goods are stocked in optimal quantities.

Automated Restocking for Continuous Supply Availability

AI streamlines **inventory replenishment** by automatically **triggering restocking orders** when inventory levels drop below a predetermined threshold. This automation:

- **Eliminates manual inventory tracking**, reducing human error.
- **Ensures consistent product availability**, preventing lost sales.
- **Improves warehouse management**, optimizing storage space.

Retail giants like **Amazon and Walmart leverage AI-driven restocking systems** to maintain real-time inventory levels, ensuring that customers can always find the products they need.

Supply Chain Optimization for Efficiency and Cost Reduction

AI enhances supply chain management by optimizing **logistics, warehousing, and distribution** processes. AI-driven supply chain solutions:

- **Identify the most cost-effective transportation routes**, reducing shipping delays.
- **Monitor supplier performance**, ensuring reliability and quality control.
- **Enhance inventory distribution across multiple warehouses**, improving delivery times.

For instance, AI-powered logistics platforms analyze **traffic patterns, weather conditions, and delivery schedules** to suggest the fastest and most efficient shipping routes, **reducing costs and improving delivery efficiency.**

2. AI-Powered Personalized Shopping Experiences

Personalization is key to improving **customer engagement and driving sales in retail and e-commerce.** AI enables businesses to offer **tailored shopping experiences, personalized recommendations, and intuitive search functionalities** that align with individual customer preferences. AI-driven personalization enhances customer satisfaction, **increases conversion rates, and builds long-term brand loyalty.**

Recommendation Engines for Smart Product Suggestions

AI-powered recommendation engines analyze **customer browsing history, purchase patterns, and preferences** to suggest relevant products. These AI-driven recommendations:

- **Encourage upselling and cross-selling**, increasing average order value.
- **Improve customer engagement**, offering personalized shopping experiences.
- **Enhance user satisfaction**, making product discovery effortless.

For example, platforms like **Amazon and Netflix use AI-powered recommendation engines** to suggest products and content based on user behavior, **boosting engagement and sales.**

Visual Search Technology for Seamless Product Discovery

AI-powered **visual search technology** allows customers to search for products using images instead of text. By analyzing images and identifying key attributes, AI-driven search engines:

- **Enhance user experience**, making it easier to find desired products.
- **Increase conversion rates**, reducing the time spent searching for items.
- **Improve search accuracy**, delivering highly relevant results.

For instance, **Pinterest and Google Lens leverage AI-based visual search tools**, enabling users to upload an image and find similar products instantly. This feature is particularly beneficial for **fashion and home decor retailers**, where visual appeal plays a crucial role in purchase decisions.

Personalized Promotions for Targeted Marketing

AI enhances marketing efforts by delivering **customized discounts, promotions, and deals** based on customer preferences. AI-driven targeted promotions:

- **Increase customer engagement**, offering deals relevant to individual shoppers.
- **Boost sales and revenue**, encouraging impulse purchases.
- **Strengthen brand loyalty**, making customers feel valued.

Retailers use AI to analyze customer data and send **personalized email campaigns, push notifications, and in-app promotions**, leading to higher **click-through rates and conversion rates**.

3. AI in Fraud Prevention for E-Commerce

With the rise of **online transactions and digital payments**, fraud prevention has become a top priority for e-commerce businesses. AI-driven fraud detection systems protect businesses and customers from **unauthorized transactions, identity theft, and fraudulent activities**. By continuously monitoring transactions and user behavior, AI enhances security and **prevents financial losses**.

Transaction Monitoring for Real-Time Fraud Detection

AI-powered fraud detection systems analyze **millions of transactions in real-time**, identifying suspicious patterns and preventing fraudulent activities before they occur. These systems:

- **Detect unusual spending behaviors**, flagging potential fraud.
- **Identify high-risk transactions**, reducing chargebacks and losses.
- **Enhance security**, minimizing unauthorized access.

For example, AI-driven fraud detection tools used by **PayPal and Stripe** continuously monitor transactions, blocking fraudulent activities while ensuring legitimate purchases go through smoothly.

Biometric Authentication for Secure Transactions

AI enhances online security through **biometric authentication methods**, such as **facial recognition, fingerprint scanning, and voice recognition**. These advanced authentication techniques:

- **Eliminate reliance on passwords**, reducing the risk of hacking.
- **Ensure secure payments**, preventing unauthorized transactions.
- **Enhance user experience**, offering frictionless authentication.

E-commerce platforms and payment gateways like **Apple Pay, Google Pay, and Samsung Pay** use AI-powered biometric authentication to provide **secure and seamless checkout experiences**.

AI-Based Anti-Fraud Systems for Identifying Suspicious Accounts

AI identifies and blocks **fraudulent accounts and suspicious activities** before they can cause harm. These AI-driven anti-fraud solutions:

- **Detect fake accounts**, reducing scams and fraudulent orders.
- **Monitor account activity**, flagging unusual login attempts.
- **Prevent bot attacks**, ensuring platform security.

For instance, AI in **eBay and Shopify helps detect suspicious accounts and fraudulent listings**, protecting both buyers and sellers from scams.

Summary

AI and cloud computing are revolutionizing business transformation by enabling intelligent analytics, automating customer interactions, enhancing financial security, and optimizing retail operations. AI-driven BI and cloud analytics empower businesses with data-driven decision-making, while AI-powered customer experience tools personalize interactions. AI enhances financial forecasting, fraud detection, and regulatory compliance, ensuring secure financial operations. In retail and e-commerce, AI-driven solutions improve inventory management, personalize shopping experiences, and prevent fraud. As AI and cloud technologies continue to evolve, their synergy will further drive innovation, efficiency, and competitive advantage in business transformation.

Chapter 9: AI in Healthcare and Cloud Computing

Introduction

Artificial Intelligence (AI) and cloud computing are revolutionizing healthcare by enhancing diagnostics, patient care, and medical research. The integration of AI with cloud-based solutions enables healthcare providers to leverage vast amounts of medical data for improved decision-making, predictive analytics, and secure data management. This chapter explores AI applications in medical imaging, electronic health records (EHR), telemedicine, drug discovery, and data security in cloud-based healthcare environments.

Cloud AI for Medical Imaging and Diagnostics

The integration of **cloud-based artificial intelligence (AI) in medical imaging and diagnostics** is transforming the healthcare industry. By leveraging AI-powered solutions, medical professionals can **detect diseases earlier, enhance diagnostic accuracy, and improve patient outcomes**. AI-driven algorithms analyze vast amounts of medical imaging data, providing **faster and more precise insights** for healthcare providers.

Cloud computing further enhances **AI-driven medical diagnostics** by offering **scalable computing power, remote accessibility, and real-time collaboration**. These innovations allow healthcare institutions to **streamline diagnostic processes, reduce human errors, and improve efficiency in disease detection**. With AI and cloud technology working in tandem, medical imaging and diagnostics are becoming **more accessible, accurate, and efficient than ever before.**

1. AI in Medical Imaging

Medical imaging plays a **crucial role in disease detection and treatment planning**, and AI has significantly enhanced its accuracy and efficiency. AI-powered solutions **process, analyze, and interpret medical images** with a level of precision that rivals human expertise, helping radiologists and healthcare professionals make **informed clinical decisions.**

AI-Powered Radiology for Enhanced Accuracy

AI-driven radiology solutions assist in analyzing medical imaging data such as **X-rays, CT scans, MRIs, and ultrasound images**. AI algorithms can:

- **Detect anomalies such as tumors, fractures, infections, and internal bleeding with high accuracy.**
- **Assist radiologists by highlighting areas of concern**, reducing diagnostic errors.
- **Accelerate image analysis**, enabling faster diagnosis and treatment planning.

For instance, **AI algorithms in radiology can detect lung nodules in chest X-rays or brain abnormalities in MRI scans,** helping doctors diagnose diseases like **lung cancer, strokes, and neurological disorders** at an early stage. AI-powered radiology tools are **particularly beneficial in emergency cases,** where rapid diagnosis can save lives.

Deep Learning in Pathology for Early Cancer Detection

AI has revolutionized **digital pathology** by using deep learning models to assist pathologists in **detecting cancerous cells with high precision**. AI-powered pathology tools:

- **Analyze biopsy samples** to identify malignant cells.
- **Reduce false positives and false negatives**, improving diagnostic confidence.
- **Enhance workflow efficiency**, allowing pathologists to focus on complex cases.

For example, AI can scan and analyze thousands of pathology slides within minutes, detecting **early signs of diseases such as breast cancer, skin cancer, and leukemia**. This speeds up the diagnostic process and improves patient outcomes by **initiating treatment sooner**.

Automated Image Segmentation for Precise Identification

AI-powered image segmentation enhances the accuracy of **medical imaging interpretation** by identifying and delineating affected areas in scans. Automated segmentation:

- **Outlines tumors, lesions, and abnormalities with precision.**
- **Improves the accuracy of treatment planning**, especially in radiation therapy.
- **Assists in monitoring disease progression over time.**

For instance, AI-powered segmentation is widely used in **oncology** to **precisely map tumor regions in MRI and PET scans**, ensuring that radiation therapy targets only the affected areas while sparing healthy tissues. This reduces side effects and enhances treatment effectiveness.

2. Cloud-Based Diagnostic Systems

Cloud computing plays a vital role in supporting AI-driven medical imaging and diagnostics by providing **scalability, accessibility, and collaboration capabilities**. Cloud-based AI solutions allow healthcare providers to **process vast medical datasets, analyze images remotely, and collaborate in real-time**, leading to more efficient and accurate diagnoses.

Scalable Computing Power for AI Processing

AI models require **high computational power** to process and analyze large medical imaging datasets. Cloud computing provides:

- **On-demand computing resources**, eliminating the need for expensive on-premise hardware.
- **Faster processing speeds**, enabling real-time analysis of medical images.
- **Cost efficiency**, as hospitals and research institutions can **scale resources as needed**.

For example, cloud-based AI solutions can analyze **thousands of MRI scans in parallel**, allowing hospitals to process patient data faster and **prioritize critical cases** for immediate intervention.

Remote Access to AI-Driven Diagnostics

Cloud-hosted AI diagnostic tools enable **radiologists and doctors to access and interpret medical images from anywhere**. This is particularly beneficial for:

- **Rural and underserved areas**, where specialist radiologists may not be available.
- **Telemedicine and virtual consultations**, allowing specialists to review images remotely.

150

- **Faster second opinions**, ensuring that patients receive the most accurate diagnosis.

For instance, a radiologist in one city can use a **cloud-based AI imaging platform to diagnose a patient in a remote area**, enabling timely medical intervention. This is especially useful in developing regions where **access to specialized healthcare professionals is limited**.

Real-Time Collaborative Diagnosis for Improved Patient Care

AI-powered **cloud diagnostic platforms** facilitate real-time collaboration between **healthcare professionals, radiologists, and pathologists**, improving the accuracy of diagnoses and treatment plans. Cloud-based collaboration tools:

- **Enable multiple specialists to review a case simultaneously**, reducing diagnostic delays.
- **Integrate electronic health records (EHRs) with AI analysis**, providing a holistic view of patient history.
- **Enhance research and innovation**, allowing institutions to share anonymized datasets for AI model improvements.

For example, **oncologists, radiologists, and pathologists can collaboratively analyze a patient's medical scans in real-time**, ensuring a comprehensive diagnosis and well-coordinated treatment plan. This interdisciplinary approach enhances patient care and treatment success rates.

AI in Electronic Health Records (EHR) and Telemedicine

The integration of **artificial intelligence (AI) in Electronic Health Records (EHR) and telemedicine** is revolutionizing modern healthcare by enhancing **efficiency, accuracy, and patient care**. AI-powered solutions are **streamlining administrative tasks, improving**

diagnostics, and personalizing treatment plans while making remote healthcare more accessible and effective.

AI in **EHR management** reduces the burden of data entry, enhances predictive analytics, and optimizes patient care through personalized treatment recommendations. In **telemedicine**, AI improves virtual consultations, assists with remote patient monitoring, and supports physicians with real-time decision-making. By leveraging AI and cloud computing, healthcare institutions can **enhance patient engagement, reduce workload for medical professionals, and ensure high-quality care.**

1. AI-Driven Electronic Health Records (EHR)

Electronic Health Records (EHR) are at the core of modern healthcare, storing critical patient data, medical histories, and treatment plans. However, **managing EHR systems manually can be time-consuming and prone to errors**. AI transforms **EHR management** by automating processes, enhancing predictive analytics, and tailoring treatment plans based on patient data.

Automating Data Entry to Reduce Administrative Workload

One of the biggest challenges in healthcare is **the time spent on manual data entry**. Doctors and healthcare professionals often spend **hours updating patient records**, reducing their focus on patient care. AI automates **data extraction, organization, and entry**, significantly reducing administrative burden.

- **AI-powered Natural Language Processing (NLP)** can extract relevant information from doctor's notes, lab reports, and prescriptions.
- **Speech-to-text AI systems** allow physicians to dictate notes, which AI then converts into structured EHR entries.

- **Automated categorization and data structuring** ensure that medical records are updated accurately and efficiently.

By eliminating **repetitive administrative tasks**, AI allows healthcare professionals to **spend more time on patient interactions and medical decision-making**.

Predictive Analytics in EHR for Proactive Healthcare

AI-driven **predictive analytics** uses patient history, lifestyle data, and genetic information to **assess disease risks and recommend preventive measures**. Machine learning models analyze **patterns in EHR data** to identify early warning signs of diseases, enabling **proactive healthcare interventions**.

- AI can **predict chronic disease progression** by analyzing past health records and lab results.
- Machine learning models assess **risk factors for heart disease, diabetes, and stroke**, prompting early interventions.
- AI-powered EHR systems can **suggest preventive screenings and lifestyle modifications** based on patient data.

For example, an AI system analyzing EHR data might **detect a patient's high risk for cardiovascular disease** and automatically schedule a preventive consultation or recommend **dietary and lifestyle changes**.

Personalized Treatment Plans for Better Patient Outcomes

AI enables **precision medicine** by tailoring treatment recommendations based on **individual patient data, genetic profiles, and medical history**. This personalization ensures that treatments are **more effective and better suited to each patient's unique needs**.

- AI-powered **decision support systems** suggest **medications and therapies** tailored to a patient's condition.

- Machine learning models analyze past treatment outcomes to **recommend the most effective interventions.**
- AI integrates with **genomic data** to provide **personalized cancer treatments and targeted therapies.**

For example, in oncology, AI-driven EHR systems can **recommend personalized chemotherapy plans** based on a patient's genetic makeup, reducing side effects and improving treatment effectiveness.

2. AI-Powered Telemedicine

The **rise of telemedicine** has made healthcare more accessible, allowing patients to consult with doctors remotely. AI enhances **telemedicine capabilities** by enabling **virtual assistants, remote patient monitoring, and AI-based decision support systems.** These innovations improve **efficiency, diagnostic accuracy, and patient engagement** in virtual healthcare.

AI Chatbots and Virtual Assistants for Patient Support

AI-driven **chatbots and virtual assistants** play a crucial role in **guiding patients through telemedicine platforms,** assisting with symptom analysis, appointment scheduling, and post-consultation follow-ups.

- **AI chatbots** use Natural Language Processing (NLP) to interact with patients, collect symptom details, and provide preliminary assessments.
- **Virtual assistants** help schedule appointments, send reminders, and guide patients through medication instructions.
- AI-powered **triage systems** determine whether a patient needs an in-person consultation or if a virtual visit is sufficient.

For example, an AI-powered chatbot can **ask a patient about flu-like symptoms,** assess severity, and suggest **a virtual doctor consultation or self-care tips,** reducing unnecessary hospital visits.

Remote Patient Monitoring for Continuous Health Tracking

AI combined with **IoT-enabled medical devices** enables **real-time remote patient monitoring**, allowing healthcare providers to track **vital signs, chronic conditions, and post-surgical recovery** from a distance.

- AI processes **heart rate, blood pressure, oxygen levels, and glucose levels** from wearable devices.
- **Early warning systems** alert doctors when a patient's health metrics indicate potential complications.
- Remote AI monitoring allows **home-based chronic disease management**, reducing hospital admissions.

For example, **diabetes patients can wear AI-powered glucose monitors** that alert doctors if blood sugar levels fluctuate dangerously, ensuring timely intervention without the need for frequent hospital visits.

AI-Based Decision Support for Physicians

During virtual consultations, AI-powered decision support systems provide **real-time diagnostic recommendations**, helping doctors **assess conditions more accurately and make informed treatment decisions**.

- AI cross-references **patient symptoms with EHR data** to suggest possible diagnoses.
- **Medical image analysis** assists doctors in interpreting **X-rays, MRIs, and lab reports** remotely.
- AI recommends **evidence-based treatment plans** tailored to the patient's condition.

For example, an AI-driven **telemedicine platform can analyze a patient's cough and fever symptoms**, compare them with similar cases, and suggest potential diagnoses such as flu or pneumonia, aiding the doctor's decision-making process.

AI-Powered Drug Discovery with Cloud-Based Computing

The process of **drug discovery and development** is traditionally a **time-consuming and costly endeavor**, often taking **years or even decades** to bring a new drug to market. However, **artificial intelligence (AI) and cloud-based computing** are transforming this landscape by **accelerating drug research, optimizing clinical trials, and enabling global collaboration**. AI-powered models analyze **massive datasets, simulate molecular interactions, and predict drug efficacy**, significantly reducing the trial-and-error approach of traditional methods. Meanwhile, **cloud computing provides the computational power and infrastructure** necessary to support AI-driven drug discovery at scale.

By integrating **AI with cloud-based computing**, pharmaceutical companies and research institutions can **discover life-saving treatments faster, lower costs, and improve patient outcomes**.

1. Accelerating Drug Discovery with AI

AI plays a crucial role in **expediting drug discovery and development** by leveraging **machine learning, deep learning, and computational biology** to analyze vast amounts of biomedical data. This approach not only **speeds up the identification of promising drug candidates** but also improves the precision and efficiency of clinical trials.

Analyzing Molecular Structures for Drug Interactions

Understanding how **new drugs interact with biological systems** is a fundamental aspect of drug discovery. AI-powered algorithms can **predict molecular behavior, simulate drug interactions, and model**

complex biochemical reactions, reducing the reliance on traditional trial-and-error methods.

- **AI-driven molecular modeling** predicts how drugs bind to target proteins, allowing researchers to refine chemical structures for better efficacy.
- **Deep learning models** analyze massive databases of molecular interactions to suggest modifications that enhance drug performance.
- AI simulates **toxicity and side effects** early in the research phase, reducing risks before clinical trials.

For example, AI-powered software like **AlphaFold**, developed by DeepMind, can **accurately predict protein structures**, helping researchers **design drugs that precisely target diseases** such as cancer and Alzheimer's.

Identifying Potential Drug Candidates Faster

Traditional drug discovery involves screening **millions of chemical compounds**, a process that can take years. AI-driven machine learning models can **analyze vast libraries of compounds and predict which ones are most likely to be effective** against a given disease.

- **Machine learning algorithms** scan through databases containing millions of chemical compounds, ranking them based on their potential efficacy.
- AI **identifies molecular patterns** associated with successful drug candidates, reducing the need for labor-intensive laboratory testing.
- **Automated drug repurposing** helps researchers identify **existing drugs** that could be used to treat new diseases, speeding up development timelines.

For instance, AI played a pivotal role in identifying **existing antiviral drugs** as potential treatments for COVID-19, significantly **shortening research timelines**.

Optimizing Clinical Trials with AI

Clinical trials are one of the **most expensive and time-consuming phases** of drug development. AI enhances clinical trials by **optimizing patient selection, predicting trial outcomes, and improving monitoring processes**.

- AI analyzes **genetic and medical records** to identify the most suitable candidates for clinical trials, ensuring better **patient stratification**.
- Machine learning predicts **which patients will respond best** to a drug, allowing for personalized treatment approaches.
- AI automates **clinical trial monitoring**, identifying potential **adverse effects early** and improving safety.

For example, AI-powered systems have been used to **match cancer patients with the most suitable clinical trials**, increasing the likelihood of successful treatments.

2. Cloud Computing in Drug Research

AI-driven drug discovery requires **massive computational power and data storage**, which is where **cloud computing** plays a transformative role. Cloud-based platforms provide **scalable, high-performance computing (HPC) capabilities**, enabling researchers to **run complex simulations, analyze large datasets, and collaborate globally in real-time**.

High-Performance Computing (HPC) for Complex Simulations

Drug research involves **running simulations of molecular interactions**, a process that demands significant computing resources. Cloud-based **high-performance computing (HPC)** solutions allow researchers to perform **millions of calculations simultaneously**, accelerating drug discovery.

- **Cloud-based AI models** process vast amounts of biological and chemical data **in hours instead of weeks**.
- HPC enables **real-time molecular dynamics simulations**, helping scientists study how drugs interact with human cells at an atomic level.
- Cloud infrastructure allows for **parallel processing**, significantly reducing the time required to test potential drug compounds.

For example, pharmaceutical companies use **Google Cloud's AI-powered computing** to conduct rapid simulations of **drug-protein interactions**, accelerating the early research phase.

Global Collaboration for Faster Drug Discovery

Cloud computing enables **global research collaboration**, allowing scientists from different institutions, companies, and countries to **work together in real-time**. This seamless collaboration accelerates the development of **life-saving treatments** and improves data sharing.

- Researchers can **access AI-powered drug discovery platforms** remotely, eliminating geographical barriers.
- Cloud-based **open-source databases** allow scientists to share research findings, reducing duplication of effort.
- Collaboration between **academia, biotech firms, and pharmaceutical companies** speeds up drug development cycles.

For instance, the **COVID-19 vaccine** was developed at an unprecedented speed partly due to cloud-based global collaboration, where researchers worldwide shared AI-driven insights and experimental data.

Big Data Processing for Identifying New Treatment Options

Drug discovery involves analyzing **huge datasets,** including genomic data, electronic health records, and clinical trial results. Cloud computing provides the necessary **infrastructure and storage** to process these datasets efficiently.

- AI-powered **big data analytics** helps identify **previously unknown drug-disease relationships.**
- Cloud storage solutions allow for **secure, HIPAA-compliant** handling of sensitive patient data.
- **Integrating genomic sequencing data** with cloud-based AI models enables the development of **personalized medicine.**

For example, cloud computing was instrumental in **sequencing the human genome,** which has paved the way for **targeted cancer therapies and precision medicine.**

Securing Healthcare Data with AI in the Cloud

The healthcare industry is increasingly adopting cloud computing to **store, manage, and analyze vast amounts of patient data.** While this digital transformation improves efficiency and accessibility, it also exposes sensitive medical information to **cyber threats, data breaches, and compliance risks.** The combination of **Artificial Intelligence (AI) and cloud-based security solutions** is revolutionizing how healthcare organizations **protect patient data, prevent cyberattacks, and ensure regulatory compliance.**

AI-driven security systems can detect **suspicious activities, automate threat responses, and enforce strict data privacy measures** to safeguard healthcare records. By leveraging **machine learning, anomaly detection, and predictive analytics**, AI enhances cloud security and ensures **secure, compliant, and resilient healthcare data management**.

1. AI for Cybersecurity in Healthcare

Healthcare data is a prime target for **hackers, ransomware attacks, and insider threats** due to its high value on the black market. **Patient records, insurance details, and medical histories** contain sensitive personal information that, if compromised, can lead to **identity theft, financial fraud, and legal consequences**. AI strengthens **cloud security** by detecting cyber threats, responding to attacks in real-time, and preventing fraudulent activities.

Anomaly Detection for Proactive Threat Identification

Traditional cybersecurity measures rely on **rule-based monitoring**, which often fails to detect sophisticated cyberattacks. AI-powered **anomaly detection systems** use **machine learning algorithms** to analyze **network traffic, user behavior, and access patterns** in real-time.

- AI continuously monitors **login attempts, file access, and data transfers** to identify **unusual activities** that could indicate a security breach.
- By recognizing **deviation from normal behavior**, AI can flag potential **insider threats, unauthorized access, or ransomware attacks** before they cause harm.
- Cloud-based AI security solutions provide **automated alerts**, enabling IT teams to **respond to threats instantly** and prevent data breaches.

For example, **IBM Watson Security and Microsoft Defender for Cloud** use AI-powered anomaly detection to safeguard **electronic health records (EHRs) and cloud-hosted patient databases.**

Automated Threat Response and Incident Mitigation

Cyberattacks in healthcare demand **rapid response mechanisms** to prevent data theft and service disruptions. AI-driven **automated security systems** can **neutralize threats in real-time** by:

- **Blocking suspicious IP addresses** attempting to access cloud-based healthcare databases.
- **Automatically isolating infected devices** to prevent malware from spreading within hospital networks.
- **Deploying real-time security patches and firewall updates** to close vulnerabilities before hackers exploit them.

AI-enhanced **Security Information and Event Management (SIEM) solutions** provide **automated incident response**, reducing the time required to detect and mitigate security breaches.

Fraud Prevention and Medical Record Integrity

Fraudulent insurance claims and **medical identity theft** cost healthcare organizations **billions of dollars annually**. AI assists in fraud prevention by:

- **Analyzing insurance claims** to detect irregular patterns that indicate potential fraud.
- Identifying **duplicate or altered medical records**, ensuring **data integrity and patient safety.**
- **Cross-referencing medical histories** to prevent **prescription fraud and unauthorized billing.**

For instance, **AI-powered fraud detection platforms** like **Shift Technology and FICO Falcon Fraud Manager** analyze vast datasets to **identify suspicious transactions and claim anomalies**, reducing financial losses for healthcare providers.

2. Compliance and Data Privacy

Ensuring compliance with **healthcare regulations** is critical to protect patient information and avoid legal penalties. AI enhances **regulatory compliance** by automating **risk assessments, enforcing data protection protocols, and monitoring access controls** in cloud environments.

HIPAA and GDPR Compliance with AI-Driven Monitoring

Healthcare organizations must comply with **Health Insurance Portability and Accountability Act (HIPAA)** in the U.S. and **General Data Protection Regulation (GDPR)** in Europe to safeguard patient data. AI helps in:

- **Real-time monitoring of cloud storage** to ensure compliance with **data retention and security standards**.
- Identifying **potential regulatory violations**, such as unauthorized access or unencrypted data storage.
- Automating **compliance reporting**, reducing the burden on IT teams.

AI-powered compliance solutions like **OneTrust and Varonis** provide **automated audits, data access logs, and regulatory tracking** to help healthcare providers meet legal requirements.

Data Encryption and Secure Access Controls

Unauthorized access to **cloud-based patient records** poses a major security risk. AI enhances **data encryption and access management** by:

- **Encrypting medical records** with **advanced cryptographic algorithms**, ensuring data remains secure even if compromised.
- Implementing **AI-driven identity verification**, such as **biometric authentication and multi-factor authentication (MFA)**.
- **Restricting access to sensitive files**, granting permissions only to **authorized personnel based on roles and responsibilities**.

For example, **Google Cloud's AI-driven security** automatically applies **end-to-end encryption** for healthcare organizations using **Google Cloud Healthcare API**, ensuring **secure data storage and transmission**.

Risk Assessment and Mitigation for Cloud Security

Cyber threats evolve continuously, requiring **proactive risk assessment** to prevent breaches. AI-powered security frameworks conduct **continuous risk analysis** by:

- **Identifying vulnerabilities in cloud storage systems** and recommending security enhancements.
- **Simulating cyberattacks (penetration testing)** to assess cloud security resilience.
- **Generating automated risk reports**, allowing IT teams to **implement preventive measures before threats escalate**.

AI-based risk assessment platforms like **Darktrace and Palo Alto Networks Prisma Cloud** provide **real-time risk analysis**, enabling healthcare providers to stay ahead of emerging threats.

Summary

AI and cloud computing are transforming healthcare by improving diagnostics, EHR management, telemedicine, drug discovery, and data security. AI-powered medical imaging enhances diagnostic accuracy, while AI-driven EHRs and telemedicine improve patient care. Cloud-based AI accelerates drug discovery, making treatments available faster. Additionally, AI strengthens cybersecurity and ensures regulatory compliance in cloud-hosted healthcare environments. The continued integration of AI in healthcare will drive innovation, efficiency, and better patient outcomes.

Chapter 10: AI and Cloud Computing in Smart Cities

Introduction

Smart cities leverage Artificial Intelligence (AI) and cloud computing to optimize urban infrastructure, improve public services, and enhance sustainability. AI-driven analytics, IoT integration, and cloud-based computing enable real-time decision-making, reducing congestion, improving energy efficiency, and ensuring smart infrastructure deployment. This chapter explores AI applications in traffic management, energy optimization, public services, and the role of Edge AI in smart city ecosystems.

AI-Driven Traffic Management and Urban Planning

As urban populations grow, cities face increasing challenges in managing **traffic congestion, public safety, and urban development**. Traditional approaches to **traffic management and city planning** often rely on **static models and outdated infrastructure**, leading to inefficiencies and rising environmental concerns. **Artificial Intelligence (AI)** is revolutionizing urban mobility and infrastructure by enabling **real-time traffic optimization, predictive analytics, and data-driven urban planning**.

AI-powered solutions enhance **transportation efficiency, reduce carbon emissions, and improve public safety** by leveraging vast datasets from **sensors, GPS, surveillance cameras, and connected devices**. Moreover, AI-driven urban planning enables cities to make **data-informed decisions** that optimize **land use, infrastructure** development, and emergency response strategies. This shift toward **AI-powered smart cities** is transforming how people commute, live, and interact with their surroundings.

1. AI for Traffic Optimization

Traffic congestion is one of the most **pressing issues in urban areas**, leading to **longer commute times, increased fuel consumption, and higher pollution levels**. AI-driven traffic management systems offer **innovative solutions** to streamline transportation networks, optimize traffic flow, and enhance road safety. By integrating **real-time data analysis and predictive modeling**, AI can significantly improve **transportation efficiency** and reduce urban gridlock.

Intelligent Traffic Signals for Real-Time Optimization

Traditional traffic signals operate on **fixed schedules**, often leading to unnecessary delays and increased congestion. AI-powered **intelligent traffic signals** use **real-time data from sensors, cameras, and GPS devices** to dynamically adjust signal timings based on **current traffic flow**.

- AI models analyze **traffic density, pedestrian movement, and vehicle speed** to optimize signal changes.
- Adaptive traffic signals help **reduce congestion at busy intersections**, improving travel times.
- AI-powered **transit priority systems** adjust signal timing for public transportation, reducing delays for buses and trams.

For instance, cities like **Pittsburgh and Los Angeles** have deployed **AI-controlled traffic signals**, reducing travel times by up to **25%** and lowering **vehicle emissions** significantly.

Predictive Traffic Management with Machine Learning

Machine learning models analyze **historical and real-time traffic data** to predict **future congestion patterns** and recommend the most efficient routes. These predictive systems assist both **urban planners and daily commuters** by:

- **Forecasting traffic surges** during peak hours, allowing authorities to implement preventive measures.
- **Optimizing traffic flow** by adjusting lane usage, toll prices, and alternative routes dynamically.
- Integrating with **navigation apps** (e.g., Google Maps, Waze) to suggest the **fastest routes** based on AI-driven predictions.

AI-powered traffic monitoring systems are already in use in cities like **Singapore and Tokyo,** where authorities rely on predictive analytics to **mitigate congestion and improve public transit schedules.**

Autonomous Vehicles and AI-Enabled Mobility

Self-driving cars are an emerging solution for **safe and efficient urban transportation.** AI enables **autonomous vehicles** to navigate city streets by **analyzing sensor data, recognizing traffic signals, and avoiding obstacles.**

- **Computer vision and LiDAR sensors** allow autonomous vehicles to detect pedestrians, cyclists, and other vehicles.
- AI-powered vehicle-to-vehicle (V2V) and vehicle-to-infrastructure (V2I) communication improves safety by sharing real-time traffic data.
- Ride-hailing services such as **Waymo and Tesla's Full Self-Driving (FSD) mode** leverage AI to provide autonomous transport options.

As self-driving technology advances, AI-driven transportation systems will play a crucial role in **reducing accidents, improving traffic efficiency, and transforming urban mobility.**

2. AI in Urban Planning

Modern cities face complex challenges related to **population growth, infrastructure development, and environmental sustainability.** AI-driven urban planning utilizes **big data, geographic information systems (GIS), and predictive analytics** to create **efficient, sustainable, and smart urban environments.**

Smart Zoning and Infrastructure Planning

Traditional city planning often struggles to balance **residential, commercial, and industrial spaces** while accommodating growing populations. AI enhances zoning and infrastructure planning by:

- **Analyzing demographic trends** to predict future housing and transportation needs.
- Identifying **optimal locations** for new roads, bridges, and public transport hubs.
- Evaluating **environmental impact** to promote sustainable urban development.

For example, AI-powered platforms like **Sidewalk Labs** use real-time data to **optimize urban zoning** and design **eco-friendly city layouts**, reducing energy consumption and traffic congestion.

Crowd Management and Public Safety

AI-driven surveillance and monitoring systems enhance **public safety and crowd management** in **high-density urban areas, transportation hubs, and large public events.** AI assists in:

- Detecting **overcrowding risks** in real-time and alerting authorities to prevent accidents.
- Analyzing **public movement patterns** to optimize pedestrian flow and reduce bottlenecks.
- Enhancing **emergency response** by deploying AI-driven security measures, such as **facial recognition and anomaly detection**.

For instance, AI-based crowd monitoring was used at the **Tokyo 2020 Olympics** to manage foot traffic, prevent congestion, and enhance overall security.

Disaster Management and Emergency Response

AI plays a vital role in **disaster prediction, response, and recovery efforts** by analyzing **climate data, geological patterns, and social media activity**. AI-driven disaster management systems help cities:

- **Predict and track natural disasters** such as hurricanes, earthquakes, and floods.
- **Optimize evacuation routes** by analyzing real-time traffic and population density.
- **Deploy emergency resources efficiently**, ensuring **first responders reach affected areas faster**.

For example, AI-powered disaster prediction tools, such as **IBM's Watson for Disaster Response**, analyze weather patterns and provide **early warnings for hurricanes and wildfires**, reducing casualties and property damage.

Cloud-Based AI for Energy Optimization and Sustainability

As the demand for **clean energy and sustainable resource management** continues to grow, cloud-based AI is revolutionizing the way energy is generated, distributed, and consumed. By leveraging **real-time data analytics, predictive modeling, and automation**, AI enhances the efficiency of **smart grids, renewable energy sources, and energy-efficient buildings**. Cloud-based AI solutions enable **scalable, cost-effective, and intelligent energy management**, helping cities, businesses, and households reduce their **carbon footprint** while ensuring **reliable power availability**.

1. AI in Smart Grid Management

Smart grids use **advanced sensors, Internet of Things (IoT) devices, and cloud-based AI algorithms** to optimize **energy distribution and consumption**. Traditional power grids often struggle with **fluctuations in energy demand, inefficiencies in power distribution, and integration challenges with renewable sources**. AI-powered smart grid management provides **real-time insights, predictive capabilities, and automated control mechanisms** to create a more **resilient, efficient, and sustainable** power infrastructure.

Demand Forecasting and Load Balancing

One of the most critical aspects of **energy optimization** is ensuring that **electricity supply matches demand**. AI-driven demand forecasting models analyze **historical consumption patterns, weather conditions, and real-time grid data** to accurately predict energy usage.

- **Utility companies** can optimize **power generation and distribution**, preventing overloads and reducing energy waste.
- AI dynamically adjusts power distribution, ensuring **efficient load balancing across the grid**.
- Cloud-based AI enables **automated adjustments in real-time**, shifting energy flows based on changing conditions.

For instance, **Google DeepMind's AI system** has demonstrated **40% energy savings** in data center cooling by predicting demand fluctuations and optimizing power consumption.

Renewable Energy Integration for a Greener Future

The growing adoption of **solar, wind, and hydroelectric power** presents challenges due to the **intermittent nature of renewable energy sources**. AI plays a crucial role in stabilizing the power grid by managing **renewable energy inputs** and integrating them efficiently with traditional power sources.

- AI models analyze **weather forecasts and energy production patterns** to determine **optimal times for renewable energy usage.**
- Intelligent energy storage solutions, powered by AI, **store excess energy during peak production times** and release it when needed.
- AI-driven microgrids ensure **reliable energy distribution** in localized areas, especially in remote or disaster-prone regions.

By using AI-powered cloud platforms, energy providers can **reduce reliance on fossil fuels, lower greenhouse gas emissions**, and improve the overall efficiency of renewable energy systems.

Automated Fault Detection and Predictive Maintenance

Power outages and infrastructure failures can lead to **significant financial losses and disruptions**. AI-driven fault detection systems continuously monitor **electrical grids, power lines, and transformers** for early warning signs of potential failures.

- AI detects **irregularities in voltage, frequency, and temperature levels** to identify possible malfunctions before they cause major issues.

- Predictive maintenance powered by AI reduces **repair costs, minimizes downtime, and extends the lifespan of grid infrastructure.**
- Automated **self-healing grids** use AI algorithms to **reroute electricity in real-time**, preventing blackouts and reducing response times to failures.

For example, **IBM's AI-powered fault detection system** helps utilities identify and fix issues before they escalate, reducing power outages and improving grid reliability.

2. AI for Smart Buildings and Energy Conservation

AI-driven cloud computing is transforming **energy management in commercial and residential buildings** by optimizing energy usage, automating climate control systems, and providing real-time analytics. Smart buildings equipped with AI-driven solutions can significantly **reduce energy costs, improve occupant comfort, and minimize environmental impact.**

AI-Optimized HVAC Systems for Energy Efficiency

Heating, Ventilation, and Air Conditioning (HVAC) systems account for **nearly 40% of energy consumption in commercial buildings**. AI-powered cloud solutions analyze **occupancy patterns, indoor air quality, and external weather conditions** to optimize HVAC performance.

- AI automatically **adjusts temperature and airflow** based on real-time data, ensuring energy is not wasted in unoccupied spaces.
- Predictive analytics help **anticipate cooling and heating needs**, preventing unnecessary energy consumption.
- AI-powered HVAC systems learn user preferences over time, ensuring **comfort while minimizing energy waste.**

Companies like **Siemens and Honeywell** are integrating AI into **smart HVAC systems**, helping businesses cut operational costs and reduce energy consumption.

Intelligent Lighting Systems for Automated Energy Savings

Lighting represents a significant portion of **electricity consumption in office buildings and urban areas.** AI-driven lighting solutions optimize energy use through **automation, motion detection, and adaptive brightness control.**

- Smart lighting systems powered by AI **automatically turn off lights** in vacant areas to reduce energy waste.
- AI adjusts lighting intensity based on **natural daylight levels,** improving energy efficiency.
- AI-integrated IoT sensors provide **real-time monitoring and adaptive control** of lighting systems across large commercial properties.

For instance, **Philips Hue and GE Current** use AI-enabled lighting solutions to reduce energy costs in **smart cities and corporate offices.**

Energy Usage Analytics and Sustainability Insights

Cloud-based AI platforms offer **real-time energy monitoring and analytics,** helping businesses and households make **informed decisions** about their energy consumption.

- AI-driven **dashboards and reports** provide **detailed breakdowns of energy usage patterns,** identifying areas for efficiency improvements.
- Machine learning models predict **peak energy consumption times,** allowing users to **optimize usage and reduce costs.**
- AI assists in **carbon footprint tracking,** helping organizations meet **sustainability goals and regulatory requirements.**

For example, **Microsoft's AI-powered sustainability cloud** helps businesses **monitor, analyze, and reduce** their environmental impact through advanced data insights.

AI and IoT for Smart Infrastructure and Public Services

The integration of **Artificial Intelligence (AI) and the Internet of Things (IoT)** is transforming urban infrastructure and public services, making cities more **efficient, resilient, and sustainable.** AI-powered solutions optimize **resource management, enhance public safety, and improve service delivery,** leading to **smarter cities that cater to the needs of growing populations.** With real-time data analytics and automation, AI and IoT enable governments and municipalities to **enhance quality of life, reduce operational costs, and promote environmental sustainability.**

1. AI-Enabled Smart Infrastructure

Urban infrastructure plays a crucial role in **sustaining modern cities,** and AI-driven IoT solutions are optimizing the way essential services are managed. By integrating **real-time monitoring, predictive analytics, and automation,** AI enhances the efficiency of **water distribution, waste management, and public safety systems,** ensuring a **more sustainable and secure urban environment.**

Smart Water Management for Sustainable Cities

Efficient water management is critical as cities face **increasing water demand and climate-related challenges.** AI and IoT technologies optimize water resources by:

- **Monitoring water consumption patterns** and detecting anomalies, such as leaks or excessive usage.
- **Predicting demand fluctuations** to ensure an **efficient and balanced** water distribution system.

- **Enhancing wastewater treatment efficiency** by automating processes and improving water recycling systems.

For instance, **IBM's AI-powered water management solutions** help cities **detect pipeline leaks, prevent wastage, and optimize water distribution**, ensuring sustainable urban water systems.

Automated Waste Management for Cleaner Cities

Traditional waste collection systems follow **fixed schedules,** leading to inefficiencies such as **unnecessary trips or overflowing garbage bins.** AI-powered **smart waste management systems** use IoT sensors and predictive analytics to **enhance collection efficiency and reduce environmental impact.**

- **IoT-enabled smart bins** detect waste levels and send real-time alerts for optimized collection.
- AI algorithms **analyze waste disposal patterns,** improving recycling efforts and reducing landfill waste.
- **Dynamic route optimization** ensures that waste collection vehicles **take the most efficient paths,** reducing fuel consumption and emissions.

Cities like **Barcelona and Singapore** have successfully implemented **AI-driven waste management systems,** significantly improving urban cleanliness and efficiency.

AI in Public Safety and Emergency Response

AI-powered surveillance and emergency response systems play a crucial role in **enhancing urban security and crisis management.** By leveraging **real-time video analytics, pattern recognition, and predictive algorithms,** AI improves public safety by:

- **Detecting suspicious activities and potential threats** using smart surveillance cameras.
- **Providing real-time alerts to law enforcement agencies** for faster response times.
- **Optimizing emergency response coordination**, ensuring first responders reach incidents quickly.

For example, **London's AI-driven security system** uses machine learning to **analyze surveillance footage**, detecting unusual behavior and potential security threats in public spaces.

2. AI in Public Services

AI is revolutionizing public services by enhancing **accessibility, efficiency, and automation**. From **citizen engagement to public transportation and infrastructure maintenance**, AI-driven solutions make cities **more responsive to residents' needs** while reducing operational costs.

AI-Powered Chatbots for Citizen Services

Government agencies and municipalities often handle **large volumes of public inquiries**, leading to delays in response times. AI-powered chatbots are transforming **citizen services** by:

- Providing **instant responses** to frequently asked questions about public policies, permits, and services.
- Offering **multilingual support**, ensuring accessibility to diverse populations.
- Automating appointment scheduling for **government offices, healthcare services, and tax inquiries**.

For instance, **Dubai's AI-driven virtual assistant "Rashid"** helps citizens navigate **government services**, reducing wait times and improving user experience.

Automated Public Transport Systems for Efficient Mobility

AI-driven public transport solutions enhance urban mobility by **optimizing transit routes, reducing congestion, and improving passenger experiences.** AI-powered systems analyze **traffic patterns, passenger demand, and weather conditions** to:

- **Optimize bus and train schedules**, ensuring efficient and timely transit.
- **Predict demand surges** to deploy additional vehicles during peak hours.
- **Improve traffic signal coordination**, reducing delays and improving road safety.

Cities like **Singapore and Helsinki** use AI-based predictive models to **streamline public transportation, reduce travel times, and enhance commuter convenience.**

Predictive Maintenance for Public Infrastructure

Aging infrastructure is a challenge for many cities, leading to **frequent breakdowns and costly repairs.** AI-driven **predictive maintenance solutions** help governments manage infrastructure **proactively** by:

- **Identifying wear and tear in roads, bridges, and public buildings** before major failures occur.
- **Reducing repair costs** by addressing issues early and preventing larger-scale damage.
- **Ensuring public safety** by monitoring **structural integrity and stability.**

For example, **New York City uses AI-based predictive analytics** to monitor subway systems, **reducing downtime and maintenance costs** while ensuring reliable transportation.

Edge AI and Cloud Synergy in Smart Cities

The rise of **smart cities** is driven by the seamless integration of **Edge AI and cloud computing**, enabling real-time data processing, enhanced decision-making, and improved urban efficiency. **Edge AI processes data locally** at the device level, while cloud computing provides **scalability, advanced analytics, and centralized coordination**. Together, they create a **hybrid AI infrastructure** that transforms urban environments into **highly responsive, secure, and intelligent ecosystems**.

1. The Role of Edge AI in Smart Cities

Edge AI plays a critical role in **smart city operations** by processing data closer to the source, reducing **latency, bandwidth usage, and dependence on cloud servers**. By enabling **real-time decision-making and automation**, Edge AI enhances city services, optimizes infrastructure, and improves safety.

Real-Time Video Analytics for Public Safety

Surveillance and security are essential components of smart cities. Traditional security systems **send video feeds to centralized servers**, leading to **delays in threat detection and high network congestion**. Edge AI addresses these challenges by:

- **Processing video analytics locally**, detecting suspicious activities, unauthorized access, and potential hazards in real-time.
- **Triggering instant alerts to law enforcement agencies**, enabling **faster emergency responses**.
- **Reducing cloud storage dependency** by analyzing video footage at the edge and only transmitting relevant data to central servers.

For example, **Singapore's AI-powered surveillance systems** leverage Edge AI to **monitor public spaces, detect anomalies, and prevent security threats** before they escalate.

Smart Traffic and Parking Systems for Urban Mobility

Traffic congestion and parking shortages are common urban challenges. **Edge AI enhances traffic flow and parking management by processing real-time data from IoT sensors and cameras.**

- **Traffic Flow Optimization**: Edge AI dynamically adjusts **traffic signals** based on congestion levels, minimizing wait times and improving road efficiency.
- **Parking Space Detection**: AI-powered **parking sensors** identify vacant spots, directing drivers through mobile applications to reduce search times and fuel consumption.
- **Incident Detection**: Edge AI detects **accidents, stalled vehicles, and road obstructions**, alerting traffic management centers for immediate action.

Cities like **Barcelona and Los Angeles** use Edge AI-driven **intelligent transportation systems** to **reduce traffic congestion and improve urban mobility.**

IoT Device Management for Smart Infrastructure

A **smart city ecosystem** relies on a network of interconnected IoT devices, including **sensors, meters, surveillance cameras, and autonomous vehicles**. Managing this vast infrastructure efficiently requires **Edge AI-driven automation.**

- **Local AI processing reduces communication delays**, ensuring IoT devices can function independently in real-time.

- **Optimized energy consumption**: Edge AI helps IoT devices operate efficiently, extending battery life and reducing power usage.
- **Seamless coordination between smart devices**: AI-powered IoT hubs analyze and relay information without **overloading cloud networks**.

For instance, **Tokyo's smart city infrastructure** employs **Edge AI to optimize energy usage, monitor environmental conditions, and enhance connectivity** across various IoT-powered public services.

2. Cloud-Edge Integration for Smarter Cities

The true potential of **smart cities** is unlocked through the **synergy between Edge AI and cloud computing**, enabling a **scalable, decentralized, and efficient AI infrastructure**. While **Edge AI enables fast, localized decision-making**, cloud computing provides **long-term data storage, large-scale analytics, and centralized system management**.

Hybrid AI Processing for Urban Efficiency

A hybrid AI model **combines Edge AI for quick decisions with cloud AI for deep insights**. This ensures cities can:

- **Handle real-time tasks at the edge**, such as **traffic control, security monitoring, and energy management**.
- **Utilize cloud AI for advanced analytics**, including **historical trend analysis, predictive modeling, and strategic urban planning**.
- **Enhance automation and self-learning capabilities**, where AI models trained in the cloud can be **deployed to edge devices for continuous improvement**.

181

For example, **London's smart grid system** employs a **hybrid AI model** to **balance energy demand in real-time while optimizing long-term power distribution** using cloud-based analytics.

Decentralized AI Networks for Enhanced Resilience

A key advantage of **Edge AI and cloud integration** is the creation of **decentralized AI networks,** improving resilience and system performance. Instead of relying on a **single centralized data center,** smart cities use:

- **Distributed AI nodes** at the edge, reducing the risk of **system-wide failures** during network disruptions.
- **Autonomous decision-making capabilities**, where edge devices can **function independently** if cloud connectivity is lost.
- **Scalable AI ecosystems,** where **new IoT devices and AI applications can be seamlessly integrated** without overloading central servers.

For instance, **San Francisco's smart city infrastructure** deploys **Edge AI-powered IoT networks,** ensuring **continuous operation even during cloud outages or cybersecurity threats.**

Data Privacy and Security in AI-Driven Smart Cities

Data security and privacy are major concerns in smart city deployments. **Edge AI enhances security by reducing reliance on centralized data centers and minimizing exposure to cyber threats.**

- **Sensitive data processing occurs locally,** preventing **unnecessary data transmission to external servers.**
- **AI-driven encryption and authentication mechanisms** safeguard IoT device communication.

- **Decentralized storage reduces the risk of large-scale cyberattacks**, as data is not **solely concentrated in a single cloud infrastructure**.

For example, **Estonia's digital infrastructure** integrates **Edge AI-based cybersecurity** to ensure **secure and privacy-compliant smart city services**, protecting citizens' data from cyber threats.

Summary

AI and cloud computing play a crucial role in transforming urban areas into smart cities. AI-driven traffic management improves mobility, cloud-based AI optimizes energy consumption, and AI-IoT integration enhances public services. Edge AI further enables real-time decision-making while working in synergy with cloud platforms. The future of smart cities lies in AI-powered, cloud-enabled solutions that enhance sustainability, efficiency, and urban living standards.

Chapter 11: AI in Cloud-Based Cybersecurity

Introduction

As cyber threats become more sophisticated, organizations increasingly rely on AI-driven cloud security solutions to enhance threat intelligence, automate responses, and strengthen overall cybersecurity resilience. Cloud-based AI enables real-time threat detection, advanced identity management, and Zero Trust security models, improving an organization's security posture. This chapter explores the role of AI in cloud cybersecurity, covering threat intelligence, identity and access management (IAM), Zero Trust models, and real-world applications.

AI for Cloud Threat Intelligence and Cyber Resilience

With the increasing adoption of cloud computing, **cyber threats have become more sophisticated**, requiring advanced security solutions to **protect sensitive data and critical infrastructures**. **Artificial Intelligence (AI) is transforming cloud security** by enabling real-time threat intelligence, predictive analytics, and automated incident response. AI-driven cybersecurity solutions empower organizations to **detect, analyze, and mitigate security threats proactively**, ensuring greater **cyber resilience and data protection**.

1. AI-Driven Threat Intelligence

AI-powered threat intelligence is revolutionizing cloud security by **analyzing vast amounts of security data, identifying vulnerabilities,**

and responding to threats in real-time. Unlike traditional security methods, which rely on **signature-based detection,** AI leverages **machine learning, behavioral analytics, and automation** to anticipate and counter cyber threats **before they escalate.**

Real-Time Threat Detection for Proactive Security

Cybercriminals continuously evolve their attack strategies, making real-time threat detection **a critical component of cloud security.** AI-driven security systems monitor cloud environments, **analyzing network traffic, system logs, and user behaviors to detect anomalies.**

- **AI-powered security tools detect suspicious activities** such as **unauthorized access attempts, data exfiltration, and unusual file modifications.**
- **Behavioral analytics algorithms establish baseline user activity,** flagging deviations that may indicate **compromised accounts or insider threats.**
- **Deep learning models improve detection accuracy** by **filtering out false positives,** ensuring that only genuine threats trigger alerts.

For example, **Microsoft Defender for Cloud** employs AI-based threat detection to **monitor cloud workloads and detect security breaches in real-time.**

Predictive Analysis to Prevent Cyberattacks

AI enhances threat intelligence by **predicting and preventing cyber threats before they occur.** Machine learning algorithms analyze **historical attack patterns,** identifying indicators of compromise (IoCs) that **signal potential future threats.**

- **Threat modeling techniques help security teams anticipate attack vectors** and reinforce cloud security measures accordingly.
- **AI-driven risk assessments analyze vulnerabilities,** providing actionable insights to **harden security defenses proactively.**
- **Continuous learning from new attack data** ensures that AI models adapt to **emerging cyber threats and zero-day exploits.**

For instance, **Google's Chronicle Security Operations** utilizes AI-powered predictive analytics to detect cyber threats **before they can cause significant damage.**

Automated Threat Hunting for Advanced Security

Traditional cybersecurity teams often struggle to **manually analyze vast amounts of security data,** leading to **delays in threat detection and response.** AI-driven **threat hunting solutions** proactively scan **cloud environments, network traffic, and endpoint activities** to uncover hidden threats.

- **AI-powered security platforms analyze real-time telemetry data,** identifying malicious behaviors before attackers exploit them.
- **Threat intelligence feeds integrate with AI models,** enabling automated **threat classification and prioritization.**
- **AI-enhanced security information and event management (SIEM) solutions** accelerate the detection of **advanced persistent threats (APTs).**

For example, **IBM Security QRadar** leverages **AI-driven threat hunting** to detect cyberattacks **before they infiltrate cloud infrastructures.**

Adaptive Security Measures for Dynamic Protection

AI enables **adaptive security frameworks** that dynamically adjust security policies based on **real-time threat assessments**. Instead of relying on **static security configurations**, AI-driven solutions continuously evolve to counter **changing attack tactics**.

- **AI-driven policy enforcement automatically strengthens security controls** when risks are detected.
- **Machine learning algorithms analyze security incidents**, recommending adaptive responses such as **restricting access to compromised cloud workloads**.
- **AI-enhanced identity and access management (IAM) systems enforce multi-factor authentication (MFA) dynamically**, tightening security based on **risk levels**.

For instance, **Amazon GuardDuty** applies **AI-driven anomaly detection** to **identify and respond to suspicious cloud activities dynamically**.

2. AI-Enabled Cyber Resilience

Cyber resilience refers to an organization's **ability to anticipate, withstand, recover from, and adapt to cyber threats**. AI-driven cyber resilience strategies **empower cloud environments** to detect, respond, and remediate security incidents **autonomously and efficiently**.

Self-Healing Systems for Automated Security Remediation

AI-powered **self-healing cloud infrastructures** automatically detect **security vulnerabilities, misconfigurations, and cyber threats**, applying **automated fixes** without human intervention.

- **AI-driven security automation tools continuously scan cloud environments,** identifying **weaknesses in configurations, access controls, and encryption policies.**
- **Autonomous remediation capabilities deploy security patches and firewall rules dynamically,** mitigating vulnerabilities before exploitation.
- **Cloud-native AI security frameworks leverage predictive maintenance,** preventing system failures and data breaches.

For example, **Google Cloud's Security Command Center** integrates **AI-driven self-healing mechanisms** to secure cloud workloads **against evolving cyber threats.**

Automated Incident Response for Faster Mitigation

Traditional incident response methods often involve **manual intervention,** leading to **delayed threat containment.** AI **accelerates incident response** by automating security actions, minimizing the impact of cyber incidents.

- **AI-powered Security Orchestration, Automation, and Response (SOAR) platforms** execute predefined **response playbooks,** containing threats automatically.
- **Automated containment actions isolate compromised cloud instances,** preventing attackers from spreading laterally.
- **AI-enhanced endpoint detection and response (EDR) solutions neutralize malware attacks,** reducing dwell time and limiting damage.

For instance, **Microsoft Sentinel** utilizes AI-driven **automated incident response** to mitigate threats **with minimal manual intervention.**

Threat Intelligence Feeds for Proactive Defense

AI integrates with **global threat intelligence platforms,** providing **real-time security insights and early warning indicators.** By analyzing **global cyberattack patterns,** AI enhances **cloud security posture.**

- **AI-powered threat intelligence platforms aggregate and analyze security data from multiple sources,** identifying global attack trends.
- **Automated threat correlation detects sophisticated attack campaigns,** enabling **proactive defense strategies.**
- **AI-driven security analytics prioritize high-risk threats,** ensuring that **security teams focus on critical vulnerabilities** first.

For example, **Palo Alto Networks Cortex XDR** leverages AI to aggregate **real-time threat intelligence,** protecting cloud environments against **evolving cyber risks.**

AI-Supported Security Orchestration for Unified Protection

AI **streamlines security operations** by **orchestrating multiple security tools, automating workflows, and enhancing coordination** among cloud security solutions.

- **AI-driven security orchestration platforms integrate firewall management, SIEM, IAM, and endpoint protection** into a single defense mechanism.
- **Machine learning-powered automation reduces alert fatigue,** allowing security teams to focus on high-priority threats.
- **AI-based correlation engines enhance visibility across cloud environments,** detecting cross-platform security incidents.

For instance, **AWS Security Hub** leverages **AI-powered security orchestration** to **unify and automate security response actions** across cloud workloads.

AI in Identity and Access Management (IAM)

Identity and Access Management (IAM) is a **critical component of cybersecurity**, ensuring that only **authorized users and devices** can access sensitive systems and data. As cyber threats grow more sophisticated, **traditional IAM methods struggle to keep up with evolving security risks. AI-powered IAM solutions** leverage machine learning, behavioral analytics, and automation to **enhance authentication, strengthen access control, and mitigate insider threats**. By integrating AI into IAM frameworks, organizations can **improve security, streamline user access, and prevent unauthorized access attempts**.

1. AI-Powered Access Control

Access control is the **foundation of IAM**, ensuring that users and devices **only access resources for which they have explicit permissions**. AI significantly enhances access control by introducing **biometric authentication, behavioral analytics, adaptive multi-factor authentication (MFA), and privileged access management (PAM)**. These AI-driven innovations **reduce security risks** while improving user convenience and operational efficiency.

Biometric Authentication for Enhanced Security

Traditional password-based authentication is **highly vulnerable** to credential theft, phishing, and brute-force attacks. AI-driven **biometric authentication** provides a **secure and user-friendly alternative**, verifying identities based on **unique physical or behavioral characteristics**.

- **Facial recognition, fingerprint scanning, and voice authentication** leverage AI algorithms to **accurately verify users in real-time.**
- **AI continuously improves biometric models,** reducing false positives and enhancing security accuracy.
- **Liveness detection** prevents spoofing attacks by distinguishing between real users and deepfake attempts.

For instance, **Apple's Face ID and Microsoft Windows Hello** utilize **AI-powered biometric authentication** to **secure user access** without requiring passwords.

Behavioral Analytics for Anomaly Detection

AI-driven **behavioral analytics** enhances IAM by continuously monitoring **user activities, device usage, and login behaviors** to detect suspicious patterns. Unlike static authentication methods, behavioral analytics **learns and adapts to each user's normal activity**, allowing it to flag **anomalous behavior that could indicate a security threat.**

- **AI detects deviations from normal user activity,** such as logins from **unexpected locations or unusual access times.**
- **Continuous monitoring enables risk-based authentication,** requiring additional verification if an activity appears suspicious.
- **AI-driven session intelligence** identifies session hijacking attempts, alerting security teams in real-time.

For example, **Microsoft Defender for Identity** and **Google BeyondCorp** use AI-based behavioral analytics to detect unauthorized access attempts **before breaches occur.**

Adaptive Multi-Factor Authentication (MFA) for Dynamic Security

Multi-Factor Authentication (MFA) is an essential layer of IAM, but **static MFA methods** can be inconvenient for users and ineffective against advanced attacks. **AI-powered Adaptive MFA dynamically adjusts authentication requirements based on real-time risk assessments.**

- **Low-risk scenarios (such as a login from a trusted device)** may require only a single authentication factor.
- **High-risk scenarios (such as login attempts from an unfamiliar location)** trigger additional verification steps, such as one-time passwords (OTPs) or biometric authentication.
- **AI continuously refines risk models** to minimize user friction while maximizing security.

For instance, **Google's Smart Lock and Okta Adaptive MFA** leverage AI-driven adaptive authentication to provide **seamless yet secure access experiences.**

Privileged Access Management (PAM) for Enhanced Security

Privileged accounts, such as **administrators and system operators**, pose significant security risks if compromised. AI-powered **Privileged Access Management (PAM) solutions** proactively **monitor, analyze, and restrict privileged access** to prevent unauthorized use.

- **AI identifies unusual privileged account activity**, such as unexpected access to sensitive systems.
- **Automated risk assessments trigger immediate access restrictions** if suspicious behavior is detected.
- **AI enforces just-in-time (JIT) access**, granting privileged users temporary access only when needed.

For example, **CyberArk and BeyondTrust** integrate AI-driven PAM solutions to **prevent unauthorized privilege escalation and insider threats.**

2. AI for Role-Based Access and Policy Management

Role-Based Access Control (RBAC) ensures that **users only have access to the resources necessary for their roles.** However, **managing user roles manually** in large organizations can lead to **overprivileged access and security gaps.** AI streamlines **role-based access and policy enforcement** by **automating role assignments, enforcing policies, enabling continuous authentication, and detecting insider threats.**

Automated Role Assignment for Efficient IAM Management

Traditional RBAC requires **manual role assignments,** which can be prone to **errors and inefficiencies.** AI simplifies this process by **analyzing user behavior, job functions, and historical access patterns** to determine the most appropriate access rights.

- **AI classifies users into roles based on machine learning analysis of job responsibilities and access patterns.**
- **Automated access reviews ensure that users do not accumulate unnecessary permissions over time.**
- **AI dynamically adjusts access rights,** granting or revoking permissions based on real-time activity.

For example, **SailPoint IdentityNow and Microsoft Azure AD Identity Governance** utilize AI-powered role management to **ensure secure and efficient access control.**

Policy Enforcement with AI to Prevent Security Violations

AI enhances **IAM policy enforcement** by ensuring that **users adhere to access control policies** while preventing privilege escalation and unauthorized access attempts.

- **AI continuously monitors access logs**, detecting policy violations such as **unauthorized attempts to access restricted data.**
- **Automated compliance checks ensure that IAM policies align with industry regulations** like **GDPR, HIPAA, and NIST.**
- **AI-driven policy automation reduces administrative overhead**, allowing IT teams to focus on more strategic security initiatives.

For example, **Google Cloud Identity and AWS IAM Access Analyzer** use AI-driven policy enforcement to **detect misconfigurations and enforce least privilege access.**

Continuous Authentication for Real-Time Identity Verification

Traditional IAM systems authenticate users **only at the time of login**, leaving security gaps for **session hijacking and unauthorized activity**. AI-powered **continuous authentication** ensures that **user sessions remain secure throughout their activity.**

- **AI constantly evaluates user behavior, device information, and network activity**, re-authenticating users if suspicious activity occurs.
- **Session monitoring prevents identity theft**, automatically logging out users if an anomaly is detected.
- **AI-enhanced authentication mechanisms prevent credential stuffing and brute-force attacks.**

For example, **Cisco Duo Security** and **Ping Identity** integrate **AI-powered continuous authentication to enhance cloud security and prevent unauthorized access.**

Insider Threat Detection to Mitigate Internal Risks

While external threats are a significant concern, **insider threats can be even more damaging**, as **malicious or negligent insiders already have legitimate access to systems.** AI helps detect **insider threats by analyzing behavioral patterns, monitoring privileged users, and identifying unauthorized data access attempts.**

- **AI detects unusual login behaviors, such as excessive data downloads or access to restricted areas.**
- **Behavioral anomaly detection alerts security teams to potential malicious insiders** before they can cause harm.
- **Machine learning models distinguish between normal and suspicious activity**, reducing false alarms while improving detection accuracy.

For instance, **IBM Security Verify and Splunk User Behavior Analytics** utilize **AI-driven insider threat detection** to **prevent data breaches and internal fraud.**

AI-Driven Zero Trust Security Models in Cloud Environments

As cyber threats grow more advanced, traditional perimeter-based security models are no longer sufficient to protect modern cloud environments. **Zero Trust Security** is a cybersecurity framework that operates on the principle of **"never trust, always verify"**, assuming that threats can originate from both inside and outside an organization's network. This model requires continuous authentication, strict access controls, and real-time monitoring of user and device activities. **Artificial Intelligence (AI) plays a crucial role in strengthening Zero Trust**

frameworks by enabling **adaptive authentication, automated threat detection, and dynamic risk assessments**. With AI-driven insights, organizations can **enhance security, reduce attack surfaces, and mitigate unauthorized access risks**.

1. AI and Zero Trust Architecture

Zero Trust Architecture (ZTA) is built on the foundation of **continuous verification, least privilege access, and micro-segmentation**. However, managing and enforcing Zero Trust policies manually can be complex and resource-intensive. AI significantly enhances the **effectiveness and efficiency** of Zero Trust by providing **automated, real-time decision-making** that strengthens security postures without adding excessive operational overhead.

Continuous Monitoring for Proactive Threat Detection

AI enables **real-time, continuous monitoring** of network activities, ensuring that access requests are **constantly assessed for potential security risks**. Unlike traditional security models that verify identities only at login, **AI-driven Zero Trust systems continuously evaluate users, devices, and applications throughout their sessions**.

- **AI-powered anomaly detection algorithms** identify deviations from normal user behavior, flagging potential security threats.
- **Machine learning models assess login patterns, session durations, and device locations** to detect suspicious activities.
- **Real-time alerts and automated response mechanisms** help security teams mitigate risks before breaches occur.

For example, **Microsoft Defender for Cloud and Google BeyondCorp** leverage AI-driven monitoring to **detect compromised credentials and unauthorized access attempts** in real-time.

Micro-Segmentation for Granular Access Control

Micro-segmentation is a core Zero Trust principle that limits access **based on user roles, device trust levels, and contextual security factors**. AI enhances micro-segmentation by dynamically **adjusting access controls** based on risk assessments, ensuring that users and devices only interact with the resources they need.

- **AI-based policy engines dynamically enforce access restrictions**, allowing only authorized interactions.
- **Network segmentation powered by AI** prevents lateral movement, restricting cyber attackers from escalating privileges.
- **Real-time visibility into user activity and device posture** ensures that only secure connections are permitted.

For instance, **VMware NSX and Illumio** use **AI-driven micro-segmentation** to **secure workloads, prevent unauthorized data access, and contain breaches** within cloud environments.

Least Privilege Enforcement for Minimizing Security Risks

The principle of **least privilege access** ensures that users, applications, and devices **only have the minimum required permissions** to perform their functions. AI automates this process by **analyzing historical access patterns and dynamically adjusting permissions based on security posture**.

- **AI-driven access management tools identify and remove excessive permissions**, reducing the attack surface.
- **Machine learning models continuously evaluate user behaviors**, revoking unnecessary privileges when risk levels increase.
- **AI-enhanced identity governance** prevents privilege escalation and insider threats.

For example, **AWS Identity and Access Management (IAM) Access Analyzer** and **Google Cloud IAM** utilize AI-based privilege management to **ensure users only have the permissions they need—nothing more, nothing less.**

Real-Time Risk Scoring for Adaptive Security Policies

AI-driven **risk scoring** evaluates users, devices, and applications in real-time, **assigning dynamic risk levels based on behavioral insights.** This enables organizations to **apply flexible security policies** that adjust automatically based on detected threats.

- **AI continuously calculates risk scores based on login locations, device health, and behavioral deviations.**
- **High-risk users or devices may be required to complete additional authentication steps**, such as biometric verification or adaptive MFA.
- **AI-driven automation allows security policies to evolve dynamically**, mitigating risks without human intervention.

For example, **Google Chronicle and CrowdStrike Falcon** leverage AI-powered risk analytics to **dynamically adjust access controls and detect advanced cyber threats.**

2. AI in Zero Trust Implementation

Implementing a **Zero Trust security model** across cloud environments requires securing **endpoints, network traffic, cloud configurations, and remote workforce access.** AI plays a crucial role in making Zero Trust implementation **scalable, automated, and intelligence-driven.**

AI-Enhanced Endpoint Security for Threat Prevention

Endpoints, including **laptops, mobile devices, and IoT systems**, are often the **weakest links in security architectures.** AI strengthens endpoint security by **continuously analyzing device behaviors, detecting anomalies, and preventing unauthorized access attempts.**

- **AI-powered endpoint detection and response (EDR) solutions** monitor processes, network connections, and file access in real-time.
- **Machine learning models detect unusual device activities**, such as unauthorized software installations or privilege escalations.
- **Automated threat containment mechanisms** isolate compromised endpoints before malware spreads.

For example, **SentinelOne and Microsoft Defender for Endpoint** use AI-driven security analytics to **protect endpoints from ransomware, phishing attacks, and zero-day exploits.**

AI-Powered Network Traffic Analysis for Intrusion Detection

Traditional **firewall-based security models** struggle to detect **sophisticated cyberattacks** that exploit cloud traffic flows. AI enhances network security by **analyzing vast amounts of data in real-time, identifying malicious activities, and blocking unauthorized connections.**

- **AI-driven deep packet inspection (DPI) identifies anomalies in network traffic,** detecting threats that traditional firewalls miss.
- **Behavioral analytics track data flow patterns**, flagging deviations indicative of data exfiltration or advanced persistent threats (APTs).
- **Automated incident response mechanisms isolate affected segments,** preventing breaches from spreading.

For instance, **Darktrace and Cisco Secure Network Analytics** leverage AI to **detect and mitigate advanced network-based threats before they cause damage.**

Cloud Security Posture Management (CSPM) for Preventing Misconfigurations

Cloud misconfigurations are a **leading cause of data breaches,** often exposing sensitive information to unauthorized users. AI-powered **Cloud Security Posture Management (CSPM)** tools continuously **scan, detect, and remediate misconfigurations in cloud environments.**

- **AI automatically detects insecure configurations, excessive permissions, and unprotected data stores.**
- **Machine learning models identify compliance violations,** ensuring adherence to regulatory standards like **GDPR, HIPAA, and NIST.**
- **Automated remediation workflows fix security gaps,** reducing human intervention.

For example, **Palo Alto Prisma Cloud and AWS Security Hub** use AI-powered CSPM to **strengthen cloud security postures and prevent data leaks.**

Zero Trust for Remote Workforces with AI-Driven Security

With **remote work becoming the norm,** securing user access **outside traditional corporate boundaries** is a significant challenge. AI-driven Zero Trust solutions ensure **secure authentication, device validation, and real-time access monitoring for remote employees.**

- **AI evaluates device health and security compliance before granting access to corporate resources.**

- **Behavior-based authentication detects anomalous remote login attempts**, preventing credential-based attacks.
- **AI-powered secure access solutions verify both user identity and device integrity**, ensuring endpoint security.

For instance, **Zscaler Zero Trust Exchange and Google BeyondCorp** use AI-driven security frameworks to **enable secure remote work without relying on traditional VPNs**.

Real-World Cybersecurity Case Studies

As cyber threats become more sophisticated, leading cloud service providers have adopted **Artificial Intelligence (AI)-driven security solutions** to safeguard their infrastructures. AI enhances cybersecurity by **detecting anomalies, predicting attacks, and automating threat responses** in real-time. Companies like **Microsoft, Google, and Amazon Web Services (AWS)** have integrated AI-powered tools into their security frameworks to **mitigate risks, enforce Zero Trust principles, and protect cloud environments** from evolving cyber threats.

1. AI in Cloud Security at Microsoft

Microsoft has **embraced AI-driven cybersecurity** to fortify its cloud platforms, including **Microsoft Azure and Microsoft 365**. By leveraging **machine learning, behavioral analytics, and real-time monitoring**, Microsoft proactively detects and neutralizes cyber threats before they can cause damage.

Microsoft Defender for Endpoint: AI-Powered Threat Detection and Response

Microsoft Defender for Endpoint utilizes **AI-based security analytics** to detect **malware, ransomware, and advanced persistent threats (APTs)**. It continuously **monitors endpoint behaviors, identifies**

suspicious activities, and automatically mitigates risks before they escalate.

- **AI-driven threat intelligence** helps detect **zero-day attacks** and previously unknown malware.
- **Behavioral-based anomaly detection** allows security teams to identify and stop insider threats.
- **Automated incident response** isolates compromised endpoints, preventing lateral movement within networks.

For example, Microsoft successfully **detected and blocked the SolarWinds supply chain attack** using its **AI-powered security analytics.**

Azure Sentinel: AI-Driven Security Information and Event Management (SIEM)

Azure Sentinel is **Microsoft's cloud-native SIEM solution** that integrates AI to provide **real-time security monitoring, threat intelligence, and automated threat response**.

- **AI and machine learning models** analyze massive amounts of security logs to **detect potential attacks** across an organization's cloud environment.
- **Automated playbooks and response mechanisms** reduce incident response times, allowing organizations to **mitigate threats faster.**
- **Integration with Microsoft Defender and third-party security tools** enhances security visibility and operational efficiency.

For instance, Azure Sentinel was instrumental in **helping financial institutions detect and prevent sophisticated phishing attacks,** reducing breach risks.

AI-Based Email Protection in Microsoft 365

Microsoft leverages AI to **protect email communications** from phishing, spam, and business email compromise (BEC) attacks.

- **AI-driven filters analyze email patterns** to detect suspicious content, links, and attachments.
- **Machine learning models adapt to evolving phishing tactics**, preventing credential theft.
- **Automated remediation features block malicious emails** before reaching users' inboxes.

Microsoft's AI-powered email security successfully **blocked over 13 billion malicious emails in 2022**, demonstrating the effectiveness of its AI-driven cybersecurity approach.

2. AI-Secured Cloud at Google

Google has implemented **AI-powered security solutions** across its cloud ecosystem, utilizing **big data analytics, machine learning, and Zero Trust frameworks** to protect businesses from cyber threats.

Chronicle Security Operations: AI-Driven Threat Detection and Forensic Analysis

Chronicle Security Operations, part of Google Cloud, applies **AI-driven analytics** to **detect and investigate cyber threats** across an organization's network.

- **AI models analyze historical and real-time security logs** to identify anomalies.
- **Threat intelligence integration** allows proactive detection of advanced cyber threats.
- **Automated forensic analysis** accelerates threat investigations, helping security teams **respond faster to incidents**.

For example, **Chronicle helped a global financial institution detect previously undetected APT activity**, preventing a potential data breach.

BeyondCorp Enterprise: AI-Powered Zero Trust Security Framework

BeyondCorp Enterprise, Google's **Zero Trust security model**, uses **AI-driven authentication** and access controls to protect sensitive data.

- **AI continuously assesses user behavior and device security posture**, ensuring only trusted users and devices can access critical applications.
- **Machine learning models detect anomalies in access requests**, blocking unauthorized access attempts.
- **Adaptive risk-based authentication** dynamically adjusts security policies based on real-time threat intelligence.

This AI-driven **Zero Trust approach** has been instrumental in **securing Google's internal systems** while also helping enterprise customers enhance cloud security.

AI-Enhanced DDoS Protection in Google Cloud

Google Cloud uses **AI-based threat detection mechanisms** to **mitigate large-scale Distributed Denial-of-Service (DDoS) attacks** before they disrupt services.

- **AI analyzes traffic patterns in real-time**, identifying and blocking malicious requests.
- **Behavioral analytics distinguish legitimate traffic from bot-driven attacks**, reducing false positives.
- **Automated threat mitigation** ensures uninterrupted availability of cloud applications.

For instance, Google successfully mitigated **one of the largest recorded DDoS attacks in history**, leveraging AI-powered defenses to **block millions of malicious requests per second.**

3. AI-Powered Security at AWS

Amazon Web Services (AWS) integrates **AI and machine learning** into its security solutions to provide **proactive threat detection, identity management, and cloud security governance.**

Amazon GuardDuty: AI-Based Threat Detection for AWS Environments

Amazon GuardDuty is an **AI-powered threat detection service** that continuously **monitors AWS accounts, workloads, and network traffic** for potential security threats.

- **AI-driven anomaly detection** identifies **unauthorized access, insider threats, and malicious activities.**
- **Machine learning models analyze millions of security events** in real-time, flagging suspicious patterns.
- **Automated threat intelligence updates** help AWS customers stay ahead of cybercriminals.

For example, AWS GuardDuty detected and stopped a **cryptojacking attack** targeting an enterprise's cloud environment, preventing unauthorized cryptocurrency mining.

AWS Identity and Access Management (IAM): AI-Driven Adaptive Authentication

AWS IAM leverages **AI-powered identity governance** to ensure **secure user access** while minimizing security risks.

- **Machine learning models detect unusual login activities**, enforcing additional authentication steps when necessary.
- **AI-driven identity analytics help organizations enforce least privilege access**, reducing the attack surface.
- **Real-time access controls adjust dynamically** based on risk factors such as location, device, and user behavior.

This AI-powered IAM solution has been widely adopted by enterprises to **prevent unauthorized access to sensitive AWS workloads.**

AI-Supported AWS Security Hub: Centralized Cloud Protection

AWS Security Hub aggregates security findings from **multiple AWS security services**, using AI to **prioritize risks and automate incident responses**.

- **AI-powered risk scoring** helps security teams focus on high-priority threats.
- **Automated remediation workflows** reduce manual security management efforts.
- **Machine learning-based policy recommendations** improve compliance and security postures.

For instance, **AWS Security Hub helped a healthcare provider strengthen its cloud security posture** by identifying misconfigurations and vulnerabilities before cybercriminals could exploit them.

Summary

AI in cloud-based cybersecurity plays a crucial role in threat intelligence, IAM, and Zero Trust security models. AI-driven solutions enhance cloud security by detecting threats in real-time, automating access control, and improving overall cyber resilience. Organizations such as Microsoft, Google, and AWS demonstrate the effectiveness of AI-powered cybersecurity in real-world applications. As cyber threats continue to evolve, AI-driven cloud security solutions will remain a key defense mechanism for businesses worldwide.

Part 4: Future Trends and Challenges

Chapter 12: Ethical Considerations in AI and Cloud Computing

Introduction

As AI and cloud computing become integral to modern businesses and society, ethical considerations must be prioritized to ensure responsible and fair technology deployment. AI models can exhibit bias, raise privacy concerns, and introduce governance challenges. Addressing these issues requires ethical AI development, strong cloud data protection measures, and adherence to regulatory frameworks. This chapter explores bias in AI models, privacy concerns, responsible AI governance, and evolving regulations in cloud computing.

Bias in AI Models and Ethical AI Development

Artificial Intelligence (AI) has transformed industries by enhancing automation, decision-making, and predictive analytics. However, AI systems are not immune to biases that can lead to **unfair, discriminatory, or unethical outcomes**. Addressing AI bias is crucial for developing **responsible, transparent, and fair AI systems** that benefit all users. Organizations must recognize the sources of AI bias and adopt ethical AI development practices to ensure **fairness, accountability, and inclusivity** in machine learning models.

Understanding AI Bias

AI bias occurs when **machine learning models produce systematically skewed or unfair results**, often reflecting societal inequalities. Bias in AI can arise from **training data, algorithmic** design, user interactions, and human decision-making. Left unchecked, biased AI systems can reinforce discrimination in areas such as **hiring, lending, healthcare, and law enforcement.**

1. Training Data Bias: The Root of AI Discrimination

AI models **learn patterns from historical data**, and if this data contains biases, the model will **inherit and amplify** those biases. For example:

- A **recruitment AI system trained on past hiring data** may favor male candidates if historical hiring trends were biased against women.
- A **facial recognition algorithm trained on limited racial diversity** may perform poorly for underrepresented groups, leading to **higher error rates in identification.**

To prevent training data bias, it is essential to **curate diverse, representative datasets** that accurately reflect the populations AI models serve.

2. Algorithmic Bias: How AI Reinforces Inequality

Even with diverse training data, **bias can still emerge due to flawed algorithmic design.** AI models rely on **weighting mechanisms, feature selection, and decision rules** that may unintentionally **favor certain groups over others**. For example:

- A **loan approval AI** that assigns higher importance to ZIP codes could **unintentionally discriminate against low-income neighborhoods,** leading to unfair credit decisions.
- A **predictive policing algorithm trained on past arrest data** may **wrongly associate specific demographics with crime,** reinforcing systemic bias in law enforcement.

To counter algorithmic bias, AI developers should **conduct fairness testing** and **use bias-mitigation techniques** such as re-weighting training data or adjusting algorithmic parameters.

3. User Interaction Bias: The Impact of Human Behavior on AI

AI models continue to learn from **user interactions**, which can introduce **new biases over time**. Recommendation engines, social media algorithms, and chatbots are **highly influenced by user behavior**.

- Search engines and **content recommendation systems** may **prioritize popular viewpoints**, suppressing minority perspectives and reinforcing **echo chambers**.
- **AI-powered hiring platforms** may develop biases based on **which candidates users engage with the most**, perpetuating **discriminatory hiring patterns**.

Regular **monitoring and retraining of AI models** can help mitigate **user-driven biases**, ensuring **fair and balanced AI recommendations**.

4. Implicit Human Bias: The Role of Developers and Data Scientists

Developers and data scientists **unintentionally introduce biases** into AI systems based on **their perspectives, experiences, and decision-making choices**. Bias can be embedded in **how data is labeled, which features are selected, and how model outputs are interpreted.**

- **A healthcare AI model** may prioritize symptoms based on data collected primarily from **male patients**, leading to **misdiagnoses for women**.

- **Facial recognition systems** may exhibit **racial or gender biases** if developers do not account for **diverse facial structures** in model training.

Organizations must **promote diversity in AI development teams** to **reduce implicit bias** and **ensure inclusive AI systems** that serve a broad spectrum of users.

Ethical AI Development Strategies

To address AI bias, organizations must **adopt ethical AI development principles** that prioritize **fairness, transparency, and accountability**. The following strategies help create **trustworthy AI systems** that align with ethical and regulatory standards.

1. Diverse and Representative Data Sets

AI models should be trained on **inclusive and balanced datasets** that **reflect diverse demographics, geographies, and social groups**. Steps to improve data diversity include:

- **Collecting data from multiple sources** to **capture variations across different populations**.
- **Eliminating historical biases** in training data by **reweighting underrepresented groups**.
- **Ensuring demographic fairness** by conducting **data audits** before AI model deployment.

For example, researchers have improved **facial recognition accuracy** by ensuring datasets contain **balanced racial and gender representations**, reducing disparities in identification accuracy.

2. Bias Auditing and Fairness Testing

Regular **bias audits and fairness testing** help detect and correct AI model biases before they cause harm. Techniques include:

- **Algorithmic fairness tests** that measure whether AI outcomes differ across demographic groups.
- **Model explainability tools** to identify which features contribute to biased decisions.
- **Impact assessments** to analyze AI model effects on **vulnerable or marginalized communities.**

For instance, **financial institutions use fairness testing** to ensure **AI-driven credit scoring models** do not **discriminate against minority applicants.**

3. Explainable AI (XAI): Enhancing Transparency

Explainable AI (XAI) ensures **AI decision-making processes are interpretable, understandable, and accountable.** XAI techniques help:

- **Increase trust in AI models** by making **decisions transparent and explainable.**
- **Allow users to challenge AI predictions** and request **human review** for critical decisions.
- **Ensure compliance with regulations** that mandate AI accountability, such as the **EU's AI Act.**

For example, AI-powered **loan approval systems with explainability features** allow applicants to **understand why their application was denied and what factors influenced the decision.**

4. Human-in-the-Loop Approach: AI with Human Oversight

A **Human-in-the-Loop (HITL) approach** integrates human oversight into **AI-driven decision-making processes**, ensuring AI does not operate **without ethical safeguards**.

- **Human reviewers validate AI-generated recommendations** in sensitive applications like **healthcare, hiring, and criminal justice**.
- **AI decisions are flagged for human intervention** when potential bias is detected.
- **Ethical review boards oversee AI deployments** to ensure alignment with fairness principles.

For example, **AI-assisted hiring tools should involve HR professionals** in final hiring decisions to **prevent discriminatory outcomes**.

5. Regulatory Compliance with Ethical Guidelines

Governments and international organizations have introduced **AI ethics guidelines** to ensure **responsible AI development**. Key frameworks include:

- **IEEE's Ethically Aligned Design**, which provides principles for developing **trustworthy AI**.
- **The European Union's AI Act**, which enforces transparency, fairness, and accountability in AI systems.
- **The U.S. AI Bill of Rights**, which outlines protections against AI-driven discrimination.

By adhering to these frameworks, companies can **reduce legal risks, enhance user trust, and ensure ethical AI deployment**.

Privacy Concerns and AI's Role in Cloud Data Protection

As cloud computing continues to evolve, artificial intelligence (AI) plays a pivotal role in managing and securing vast amounts of data. Organizations rely on AI-driven cloud systems to process and analyze data efficiently, but this advancement also introduces significant privacy risks. The integration of AI in cloud environments raises concerns about unauthorized access, data misuse, and user transparency, making it essential to implement robust privacy protection mechanisms.

AI's Impact on Data Privacy

AI-powered cloud platforms handle **massive volumes of personal and sensitive information**, making them a prime target for cyber threats and regulatory scrutiny. While AI enhances automation and decision-making, it also introduces risks that could compromise user privacy.

Data Breaches: A Growing Concern

With cloud environments housing vast amounts of data, **AI-driven cyberattacks** have become more sophisticated. Cybercriminals exploit vulnerabilities in cloud security to gain unauthorized access to sensitive information, leading to large-scale **data breaches**. AI-powered **malware and ransomware** attacks can evade traditional security measures, exfiltrating personal data and corporate secrets. If organizations fail to implement strong **AI-based encryption and anomaly detection systems**, they risk exposing critical data to cyber threats.

Unauthorized Data Collection and Ethical Concerns

AI algorithms continuously learn and improve by processing vast datasets, but this capability can lead to **unauthorized data collection**. Many AI-powered cloud applications **harvest personal information** from users without explicit consent, raising ethical and legal concerns. Companies may collect **location data, browsing habits, financial**

215

records, and health information without fully disclosing their data collection policies. This lack of transparency can result in **privacy violations** and non-compliance with regulations like the **General Data Protection Regulation (GDPR) and the California Consumer Privacy Act (CCPA)**.

Profiling and Surveillance Risks

AI systems in cloud environments create **detailed user profiles** by analyzing behavioral patterns, preferences, and interactions. While profiling enhances user experiences by offering **personalized recommendations**, it also poses **privacy risks**. Governments and corporations can leverage AI-powered profiling for **mass surveillance**, potentially infringing on individuals' privacy rights. AI-driven monitoring tools in cloud platforms may track employee productivity, customer behavior, or user activities, leading to **ethical dilemmas about data ownership and consent**.

Lack of Transparency in AI Decision-Making

Many AI-driven cloud applications operate as **black-box systems**, making it difficult for users to understand how their data is processed, stored, and used. This lack of transparency raises concerns about **AI decision-making in financial services, healthcare, hiring, and law enforcement**. If users and regulatory bodies cannot audit AI models for **fairness and accuracy**, organizations risk losing **customer trust and facing legal challenges**. Companies must implement **explainable AI (XAI) techniques** to ensure their cloud AI systems operate with transparency and accountability.

AI-Driven Cloud Security Solutions

Despite these privacy concerns, AI serves as a powerful tool for **enhancing cloud data protection**. By leveraging AI-driven security solutions, organizations can **proactively identify, mitigate, and**

prevent cyber threats while ensuring compliance with privacy regulations.

AI-Powered Encryption for Secure Data Storage and Transmission

AI enhances encryption techniques by dynamically adapting **cryptographic protocols** to protect data **at rest, in transit, and in use**. AI-driven encryption algorithms detect vulnerabilities in traditional security models and **automatically adjust encryption keys** to prevent unauthorized decryption. Additionally, **homomorphic encryption** allows AI models to perform computations on encrypted data, preserving privacy without exposing sensitive information.

Anomaly Detection and Threat Prevention

AI-driven **anomaly detection systems** analyze real-time data patterns to identify **unusual access behavior** and detect potential **cybersecurity threats**. Unlike traditional security measures that rely on predefined rules, AI continuously **learns from evolving attack patterns** and responds to threats before they escalate. **Behavioral analytics, machine learning-based intrusion detection, and AI-powered Security Information and Event Management (SIEM) tools** enable organizations to prevent data breaches and unauthorized intrusions in cloud environments.

AI-Driven Identity and Access Management (IAM)

Identity and Access Management (IAM) systems powered by AI **enforce strict access policies** by continuously **verifying user identities and monitoring access privileges**. AI-driven IAM uses techniques such as **multi-factor authentication (MFA), biometric authentication, and risk-based access controls** to ensure only **authorized users** can access sensitive data. By leveraging AI, organizations can **dynamically adjust access permissions** based on real-time risk assessments, minimizing the threat of **insider attacks and account takeovers**.

Privacy-Preserving AI Techniques

To address growing privacy concerns, organizations are adopting **privacy-preserving AI techniques** such as **federated learning and differential privacy.**

- **Federated Learning:** This approach allows AI models to **train on decentralized data** without requiring direct access to user information. Instead of sending raw data to a centralized server, federated learning enables models to learn from distributed sources, ensuring **data privacy** while maintaining accuracy.
- **Differential Privacy:** AI models equipped with differential privacy techniques **add noise to datasets**, preventing individual data points from being traced back to specific users. This approach enables organizations to **analyze trends and patterns** without compromising user privacy.

Responsible AI and Cloud Governance

As artificial intelligence (AI) continues to shape cloud computing and digital transformation, **responsible AI governance** has become essential for ensuring ethical, fair, and secure AI deployment. AI-powered cloud systems process vast amounts of sensitive data, automate critical decisions, and influence business and societal outcomes. Without strong governance frameworks, these technologies risk **exacerbating biases, infringing on user privacy, and creating security vulnerabilities**. Responsible AI governance establishes principles and best practices that guide organizations in **developing, deploying, and monitoring AI-driven cloud solutions** while aligning with ethical, regulatory, and societal expectations.

Principles of Responsible AI Governance

Governance frameworks provide a structured approach to managing AI and cloud computing systems, ensuring that these technologies are deployed **transparently, fairly, and securely**. The core principles of responsible AI governance include:

Transparency: Ensuring Explainability and Open AI Practices

One of the fundamental principles of responsible AI governance is **transparency**. Organizations must disclose how **AI models operate, what data they use, and how decisions are made**. AI-driven cloud solutions should be designed with **explainability in mind**, allowing users and stakeholders to **understand AI-generated outputs**. Implementing **explainable AI (XAI)** techniques ensures that decisions made by AI models can be audited, reducing the risks associated with opaque, black-box AI systems. Transparency fosters **trust among users, regulators, and businesses**, ensuring ethical AI deployment in cloud environments.

Accountability: Establishing Clear Responsibility Structures

AI governance frameworks should define **who is responsible** for AI-related outcomes. Organizations must establish clear accountability structures, ensuring that AI developers, data scientists, and cloud service providers adhere to **ethical and legal standards**. Implementing **governance policies that specify AI model ownership, decision oversight, and risk management procedures** ensures that AI systems operate responsibly. Furthermore, organizations must be **prepared to address unintended consequences**, such as biased decision-making or security breaches, by establishing mechanisms for **redress and correction**.

Fairness: Mitigating AI Bias and Promoting Inclusivity

AI-driven cloud solutions must be **fair and unbiased** to prevent discrimination against individuals or groups. Bias in AI models can arise from **skewed training data, algorithmic limitations, or human oversight failures**. Responsible AI governance requires organizations to implement **bias detection and fairness audits** to evaluate AI models for **potential discriminatory patterns**. Ensuring fairness in AI systems helps prevent **discriminatory hiring practices, biased financial assessments, and unequal access to digital services**. By using **diverse and representative datasets**, organizations can promote **inclusivity and equity in AI decision-making**.

Security and Reliability: Safeguarding AI Systems Against Threats

AI models integrated with cloud computing must be **secure and reliable** to prevent **manipulation, adversarial attacks, or unintended failures**. AI governance frameworks emphasize **strong cybersecurity measures**, including **data encryption, multi-factor authentication, and anomaly detection** to **protect AI-driven cloud applications from cyber threats**. Organizations should implement **continuous monitoring and real-time threat intelligence** to ensure that AI systems remain resilient against emerging risks. Additionally, responsible AI governance ensures that **AI models are consistently updated, tested, and validated** to maintain their reliability and effectiveness in cloud environments.

Best Practices for AI and Cloud Governance

To uphold responsible AI governance, organizations must adopt **proactive measures** to ensure compliance with ethical standards, industry regulations, and evolving AI policies. Key best practices include:

Establishing AI Ethics Committees

Organizations should create **AI ethics committees** or advisory boards to **oversee AI deployment and governance**. These committees consist of **AI experts, ethicists, legal professionals, and stakeholders** who assess AI models for potential **biases, security risks, and regulatory compliance issues**. By fostering **multidisciplinary oversight**, ethics committees ensure that AI and cloud services align with organizational values and **global ethical guidelines**, such as the **EU AI Act and IEEE's Ethically Aligned Design framework**.

Continuous AI Auditing and Monitoring

AI-driven cloud systems should undergo **continuous monitoring and auditing** to ensure compliance with **ethical, security, and performance standards**. AI auditing tools analyze **algorithmic decisions, model performance, and bias tendencies** to detect **unintended consequences or potential ethical violations**. Organizations should also implement **real-time AI monitoring solutions** that track how AI models evolve over time, ensuring they remain **aligned with ethical principles and regulatory standards**. Regular **audits and risk assessments** help organizations **identify and mitigate AI-related issues before they impact users or businesses**.

Implementing User Consent Mechanisms

User autonomy and data privacy are critical aspects of responsible AI governance. Organizations should implement **user consent mechanisms** that allow individuals to **control how their data is collected, processed, and shared by AI-powered cloud systems**. Features such as **opt-in and opt-out functionalities, data anonymization, and customizable privacy settings** empower users to make informed decisions about their data interactions. Ensuring **compliance with privacy laws like GDPR and CCPA** helps organizations **build trust and maintain ethical AI practices**.

Collaborating with Regulatory Bodies and Policymakers

To align AI and cloud services with evolving legal requirements, organizations should collaborate with **regulatory bodies, industry leaders, and government agencies**. Engaging with policymakers helps businesses stay **up to date with AI governance regulations** and adopt industry best practices. Organizations should participate in **global AI** governance initiatives, contribute to **ethical AI research**, and **advocate for responsible AI development**. Proactive collaboration ensures that AI systems remain **compliant with ethical standards and legal mandates** while fostering innovation in cloud computing.

Regulatory Compliance and Future Policies in AI and Cloud Computing

As AI and cloud computing continue to advance, governments and regulatory bodies worldwide are **establishing and refining policies** to ensure data security, privacy, and ethical AI usage. These regulations are critical in addressing the **growing concerns over AI-driven decision-making, data protection, and cybersecurity threats**. Organizations operating in cloud environments must **adhere to evolving compliance requirements** to avoid legal repercussions and maintain trust with users.

Key AI and Cloud Regulations

Regulatory frameworks play a crucial role in **governing how AI technologies interact with cloud computing infrastructures**. Several key regulations have been established to **protect data privacy, ensure AI fairness, and mitigate cybersecurity risks**.

General Data Protection Regulation (GDPR)

The **General Data Protection Regulation (GDPR)** is one of the most comprehensive data protection laws in the world, governing **organizations operating within the European Union (EU) and those handling EU citizens' data**. GDPR mandates strict compliance measures, including **user consent for data collection, the right to data erasure, and stringent data breach reporting requirements**. AI-powered cloud systems processing personal data must ensure **compliance with GDPR's principles of transparency, accountability, and data minimization**. Non-compliance can result in severe penalties, including **fines of up to 4% of a company's global annual revenue.**

California Consumer Privacy Act (CCPA)

The **California Consumer Privacy Act (CCPA)** is the **U.S. equivalent of GDPR,** granting California residents greater control over their personal data. Organizations collecting or processing **California consumers' data must provide transparency on how data is used, allow users to opt out of data sales, and ensure data protection measures.** AI-driven cloud solutions must comply with CCPA by implementing **robust privacy controls** that enable users to **manage their data access rights effectively.**

NIST AI Risk Management Framework

The **National Institute of Standards and Technology (NIST) AI Risk Management Framework** provides **guidelines for developing trustworthy AI systems.** This framework helps organizations address risks associated with **bias, transparency, robustness, and security in AI models.** Cloud providers integrating AI technologies are encouraged to adopt **NIST's best practices for risk assessment, data protection, and AI explainability** to **enhance system reliability and ethical AI deployment.**

EU AI Act

The **EU AI Act** is a landmark regulation designed to **establish legal requirements for AI safety, transparency, and fairness.** It categorizes AI applications into **risk-based tiers,** including **prohibited, high-risk, and low-risk AI systems.** AI-driven cloud services used in critical sectors—such as **healthcare, finance, and public administration—must meet stringent requirements related to bias prevention, transparency, and human oversight.** The EU AI Act aims to create a standardized **regulatory framework** that balances **innovation with ethical AI governance.**

ISO/IEC 27001: Cloud Security Standard

ISO/IEC 27001 is an **international standard for information security management systems (ISMS)**, ensuring **data confidentiality, integrity, and availability** in cloud environments. Organizations adopting AI-driven cloud solutions must **comply with ISO/IEC 27001** by implementing **comprehensive security measures, risk assessments, and incident response strategies.** Adherence to this standard helps businesses **strengthen their cloud security posture while meeting regulatory expectations.**

Future Trends in AI and Cloud Compliance

Regulatory frameworks will continue to evolve as AI and cloud computing **introduce new challenges related to privacy, security, and ethical responsibility.** Several key trends will shape the future of **AI and cloud compliance.**

Stronger Global AI Governance

As AI adoption grows, governments and international organizations are **collaborating to develop unified AI governance frameworks.** Future regulations may focus on **establishing global AI safety standards, ethical AI principles, and standardized risk management approaches.** Cross-border data-sharing agreements and **international AI oversight committees** may emerge to ensure AI technologies remain **accountable and beneficial to society.**

More Stringent Data Protection Laws

To address the increasing risks of **AI-driven data privacy violations,** future data protection laws will likely **introduce stricter compliance**

measures. Governments may require AI-powered cloud platforms to implement **advanced data anonymization techniques, enhanced encryption protocols, and stronger user consent mechanisms.** Additionally, **penalties for data breaches and AI misuse may become more severe,** encouraging businesses to prioritize **AI security and responsible data handling.**

Mandatory AI Impact Assessments

Organizations deploying AI-driven cloud services may soon be required to conduct **mandatory AI impact assessments** before launching new AI applications. These assessments will evaluate:

- **Potential biases in AI models**
- **Security vulnerabilities**
- **Privacy risks associated with data processing**
- **Compliance with ethical AI standards**

By implementing **AI risk assessments,** businesses can proactively identify and mitigate AI-related risks, **ensuring compliance with evolving legal and ethical guidelines.**

Automated Regulatory Compliance Tools

AI itself is becoming a **powerful tool for regulatory compliance.** Organizations are adopting **AI-driven compliance monitoring solutions** that:

- **Automatically detect non-compliance issues in cloud environments**
- **Analyze regulatory changes in real-time**
- **Generate compliance reports and risk assessments**

These AI-powered compliance tools enhance **regulatory adherence, reduce human error, and streamline legal compliance processes** for businesses operating in cloud-based AI ecosystems.

Summary

Ethical considerations in AI and cloud computing are essential to ensuring fairness, transparency, and compliance with regulatory standards. Addressing AI bias, enhancing data privacy, implementing responsible governance, and adhering to global policies are key factors in ethical AI deployment. As AI and cloud computing continue to advance, organizations must adopt ethical frameworks to build trust and ensure responsible innovation.

Chapter 13: The Future of AI in Cloud Computing

Introduction

The integration of artificial intelligence (AI) and cloud computing is shaping the future of technology, enabling advanced automation, enhanced security, and optimized resource management. Emerging trends such as autonomous cloud platforms, self-healing infrastructure, quantum computing, and AI-driven predictions will transform the way organizations deploy and manage cloud environments. This chapter explores these advancements and their potential impact on the future of cloud computing.

The Rise of AI-Powered Autonomous Cloud Platforms

Cloud computing has undergone a significant transformation with the integration of **Artificial Intelligence (AI) and Machine Learning (ML)**. Traditional cloud management required extensive **manual intervention for provisioning, monitoring, and optimization**, but AI-powered **autonomous cloud platforms** are revolutionizing the way businesses manage their cloud environments. These platforms leverage **advanced automation, predictive analytics, and intelligent security** to enhance **efficiency, scalability, and reliability** while reducing operational costs.

What Are Autonomous Cloud Platforms?

Autonomous cloud platforms are AI-driven **self-managing cloud environments** that automate the **deployment, management, and**

optimization of cloud resources with minimal human intervention. By utilizing AI and ML, these platforms can **dynamically adjust resource allocation, optimize workloads, and enhance security** without requiring constant manual oversight.

These intelligent cloud systems bring numerous advantages, including:

- **Operational Efficiency** – AI-driven automation reduces the need for manual configurations, minimizing human errors and improving **workforce productivity.**
- **Cost Optimization** – AI continuously monitors resource utilization and **adjusts scaling dynamically**, ensuring businesses only pay for what they use.
- **Enhanced Reliability** – AI-powered platforms **predict failures before they occur** and automatically take corrective actions, leading to improved system uptime.
- **Security and Compliance** – AI-driven security mechanisms **detect anomalies in real-time**, preventing potential cyber threats and ensuring regulatory compliance.

By leveraging AI, **autonomous cloud platforms enable businesses to focus on innovation** rather than spending time on repetitive cloud management tasks.

Features of AI-Driven Autonomous Clouds

AI-powered autonomous cloud platforms are built with **advanced capabilities** that transform traditional cloud management into a more **intelligent and automated** system. Some of the key features include:

1. Automated Provisioning

AI automates the **allocation and scaling of cloud resources** based on real-time workload demands. Traditional cloud environments required **manual intervention to scale up or down**, but AI-driven platforms analyze historical data and **predict when additional resources are needed**. This results in **efficient resource utilization, reduced latency, and seamless performance** across applications.

2. Predictive Analytics for Performance Optimization

One of the major advantages of AI in cloud computing is its ability to **analyze vast amounts of operational data** and provide **predictive insights**. AI-powered autonomous clouds monitor **system performance, user behavior, and traffic patterns** to anticipate **potential failures or inefficiencies**. This allows organizations to **prevent downtime, reduce service disruptions, and optimize workloads** proactively.

For example, AI-driven predictive analytics can detect an **increasing load on an e-commerce platform** during a sale event and **automatically provision additional computing resources** before performance degradation occurs.

3. Intelligent Security Management

Security remains a **top priority** in cloud computing, and AI enhances cloud security by continuously **monitoring, analyzing, and responding to cyber threats** in real-time. AI-driven security features include:

- **Anomaly Detection** – AI identifies unusual behavior, such as unauthorized access attempts or abnormal data transfers, and alerts administrators or takes **automated corrective actions**.
- **Threat Intelligence** – AI-powered systems integrate with global threat intelligence databases to recognize **emerging cyber threats** and automatically apply security measures.
- **Automated Compliance Enforcement** – AI ensures that cloud resources **adhere to regulatory standards**, such as **GDPR, CCPA, and ISO 27001**, reducing compliance risks.

4. Self-Optimizing Workloads

AI-driven autonomous cloud platforms are designed to continuously **analyze workload performance and adjust configurations** to maintain **optimal efficiency.** These platforms leverage **real-time monitoring and machine learning algorithms** to dynamically allocate computing power, storage, and network resources based on application needs.

For instance, AI can detect a **database query bottleneck in a cloud application** and automatically optimize indexing or reallocate resources to improve performance **without human intervention.**

Leading Autonomous Cloud Platforms

Several major cloud providers have embraced AI to **enhance automation and intelligence in cloud management.** These platforms incorporate **AI-driven automation, security, and optimization tools** to provide businesses with a **scalable and resilient cloud infrastructure.**

1. AWS Auto Scaling and AI-Powered Optimization Tools

Amazon Web Services (AWS) offers **AI-driven automation tools** that allow organizations to efficiently **scale cloud resources and optimize workloads.**

- **AWS Auto Scaling** automatically adjusts compute resources based on real-time demand, ensuring cost-efficiency and high availability.
- **Amazon SageMaker** enables businesses to build and deploy **machine learning models within AWS cloud environments** for predictive analytics and automation.

- **AWS Security Hub** utilizes AI-powered security intelligence to detect and **mitigate potential cyber threats** across cloud workloads.

2. Azure AI-Based Cloud Governance

Microsoft Azure integrates AI into its cloud governance and management solutions to provide businesses with **enhanced security, compliance, and performance optimization.**

- **Azure Machine Learning** enables organizations to train AI models that enhance **cloud automation and decision-making**.
- **Azure Security Center** leverages AI for **real-time threat detection and risk assessments**, helping enterprises secure their cloud infrastructure.
- **Azure Auto-Scaling Solutions** allow applications to dynamically scale based on workload variations, improving efficiency and cost-effectiveness.

3. Google Cloud's AI-Driven Workload Management

Google Cloud has developed AI-powered automation solutions that **optimize cloud operations, enhance security, and streamline performance.**

- **Google Cloud Operations (formerly Stackdriver)** uses AI for real-time **performance monitoring, logging, and diagnostics**.
- **Google Cloud AutoML** simplifies **machine learning model deployment**, making AI-driven automation accessible to businesses.
- **AI-Powered Cost Optimization** tools help organizations reduce cloud spending by **analyzing resource usage and providing cost-saving recommendations**.

AI-Driven Self-Healing Cloud Infrastructure

Cloud computing has become the backbone of modern digital transformation, but with increasing complexity, managing cloud environments manually can be challenging. **AI-driven self-healing cloud infrastructure** is emerging as a game-changer, offering businesses the ability to detect, diagnose, and resolve issues **autonomously**. By leveraging artificial intelligence, machine learning, and automation, **self-healing cloud systems ensure high availability, resilience, and optimized performance** without human intervention. This approach minimizes downtime, reduces operational costs, and enhances overall system security, making it an essential advancement in cloud technology.

Understanding Self-Healing Cloud Infrastructure

Self-healing cloud infrastructure is designed to **proactively manage system failures, performance issues, and security threats** by utilizing AI and automation. Unlike traditional cloud environments that require **manual troubleshooting and intervention**, self-healing systems detect problems **in real-time** and apply automated corrective actions to **prevent service disruptions**.

A **self-healing cloud system** continuously monitors cloud resources, identifying anomalies, hardware failures, or configuration errors. Once an issue is detected, AI-driven automation responds immediately by **restarting, reconfiguring, or scaling resources as needed**. This proactive approach ensures that **cloud services remain available, reliable, and resilient**, even in the face of unexpected failures.

By implementing **self-healing capabilities**, cloud providers and enterprises can eliminate the risks associated with **manual errors, delayed incident response, and prolonged downtime**. This intelligent cloud infrastructure enhances business continuity, making it a critical component for industries that rely on **real-time applications, e-**

commerce platforms, financial services, and mission-critical workloads.

Key Technologies Enabling Self-Healing Clouds

AI-powered self-healing cloud infrastructure relies on several advanced technologies that enable **real-time detection, automated resolution, and predictive analytics** to maintain seamless cloud operations. Some of the key technologies driving self-healing capabilities include:

1. Machine Learning for Anomaly Detection

Machine learning (ML) plays a crucial role in identifying **irregular patterns in system behavior** that could indicate potential failures or security threats. By analyzing historical and real-time data, **ML algorithms can predict system anomalies** and alert the cloud infrastructure before an issue escalates.

For instance, if an AI-driven monitoring system detects **unusual spikes in CPU usage, memory leaks, or network latency**, it can take proactive steps such as **reallocating resources, isolating the issue, or notifying administrators** before the performance degrades. This predictive approach helps minimize **unexpected downtime and system failures**.

2. Automated Incident Resolution

AI-driven automation enables **self-healing cloud environments** to take immediate corrective actions without human intervention. When an issue is detected, automated incident resolution tools can:

- Restart cloud instances
- Scale resources dynamically
- Apply configuration changes
- Redirect traffic to healthy nodes

- Implement automated failover mechanisms

For example, if a **virtual machine (VM) crashes**, AI-powered automation can detect the failure and instantly **provision a new VM instance** to maintain service continuity. This reduces the need for manual intervention, ensuring a **faster recovery time**.

3. Predictive Maintenance

Traditional IT infrastructure relies on **reactive maintenance**, where issues are addressed **after they occur**. In contrast, self-healing cloud infrastructure leverages **AI-driven predictive maintenance** to anticipate hardware or software failures before they happen.

By analyzing historical data, AI can identify patterns indicating **potential hardware degradation**, such as disk failures, network congestion, or memory leaks. Based on these insights, the system can **schedule preventive maintenance**, ensuring that cloud resources remain **functional and optimized**.

For instance, if AI detects signs of an imminent **server failure**, it can migrate workloads to a **healthy server before the failure impacts users**, thereby preventing downtime and ensuring seamless cloud operations.

4. Intelligent Load Balancing

AI-powered load balancing dynamically distributes workloads across cloud resources to **optimize performance, prevent overloads, and minimize downtime**. Traditional load balancers distribute traffic based on predefined rules, but AI-driven load balancing **analyzes real-time workload patterns** and makes **adaptive decisions** to maintain efficiency.

If a **specific cloud server is experiencing high traffic**, AI-powered load balancing can **reroute requests to underutilized servers** to maintain **optimal response times**. Additionally, AI can predict traffic spikes and **scale resources dynamically**, ensuring a smooth user experience **even during peak demand periods**.

Benefits of AI-Powered Self-Healing Infrastructure

AI-driven self-healing cloud infrastructure provides a wide range of benefits for businesses looking to optimize **performance, security, and operational efficiency**. Some of the key advantages include:

1. Reduced Downtime

One of the most significant benefits of self-healing cloud infrastructure is its ability to **prevent system failures before they escalate**. Traditional cloud management requires **manual intervention to troubleshoot issues**, which can lead to prolonged downtime. AI-driven automation ensures that **issues are detected and resolved in real-time**, minimizing service disruptions.

For example, in an **e-commerce platform**, if AI detects a **slow database query affecting checkout speed**, it can automatically **optimize indexing, allocate more resources, or reroute requests** to improve performance without impacting customers.

2. Lower Operational Costs

By automating cloud management and incident resolution, AI-powered self-healing infrastructure reduces the **need for manual intervention**, lowering operational expenses. IT teams no longer have to spend **time manually diagnosing and fixing cloud issues,** allowing them to focus on more strategic initiatives.

Additionally, AI-driven **predictive maintenance and intelligent scaling** ensure that businesses only use the **necessary amount of cloud resources**, eliminating **unnecessary cloud spending**. This results in **better cost efficiency and optimized resource utilization**.

3. Enhanced Security and Threat Mitigation

Security remains a top concern for cloud environments, and AI-driven self-healing infrastructure enhances **real-time threat detection and response**. AI continuously monitors **network traffic, user behavior, and access logs** to detect anomalies that could indicate **cyber threats, unauthorized access, or potential security breaches**.

For instance, if an AI-powered **intrusion detection system** identifies an unusual login attempt from an unrecognized device, it can **automatically block access, alert security teams, or enforce multi-factor authentication (MFA)** to prevent unauthorized access.

Additionally, self-healing security mechanisms can **patch vulnerabilities automatically**, ensuring that cloud environments remain **protected against emerging cyber threats**.

The Impact of Quantum Computing on AI in the Cloud

The convergence of **quantum computing, artificial intelligence (AI), and cloud computing** is set to redefine the future of technology. As businesses and researchers push the boundaries of AI-driven solutions, quantum computing emerges as a **revolutionary force capable of processing vast datasets and solving complex problems** at unprecedented speeds. The impact of quantum computing on AI in the cloud extends to **faster model training, enhanced security, improved resource management, and groundbreaking AI algorithms**. However, challenges such as **hardware limitations, security risks, and integration complexities** remain barriers to widespread adoption.

What is Quantum Computing?

Quantum computing leverages the principles of **quantum mechanics**, such as **superposition and entanglement,** to perform calculations that would take traditional computers **millions of years** to solve. Unlike classical computers that process data in binary (0s and 1s), quantum computers use **qubits**, which can exist in multiple states simultaneously. This unique ability enables quantum computers to perform **parallel computations** and analyze complex data structures exponentially faster than conventional computing systems.

In the context of **AI and cloud computing**, quantum computing presents an opportunity to **overcome the limitations of classical hardware**. AI models often require **massive computational power** for training, especially in areas such as **deep learning, natural language processing (NLP), and real-time data analysis**. Quantum computing has the potential to **accelerate AI advancements** by reducing processing times, optimizing decision-making models, and enhancing cloud-based AI applications.

How Quantum Computing Enhances AI and Cloud Computing

The integration of quantum computing with AI in the cloud unlocks new capabilities that could **revolutionize industries such as finance, healthcare, cybersecurity, and logistics.** Several key areas highlight how quantum computing enhances **AI and cloud computing**:

1. Accelerated AI Model Training

AI and machine learning models require significant **computational resources** to process and analyze large datasets. Traditional GPUs and CPUs, while powerful, often struggle with **high-dimensional data and deep learning models**, leading to extended training times. Quantum computing introduces a paradigm shift by enabling **parallel processing on an unprecedented scale**, significantly reducing AI training times.

For example, quantum algorithms like **Quantum Approximate Optimization Algorithm (QAOA)** and **Variational Quantum Eigensolver (VQE)** are being explored to solve **complex machine learning problems** that classical systems find intractable. This advancement allows AI models to **learn faster, recognize patterns more effectively, and improve decision-making accuracy**.

2. Enhanced Cryptographic Security

Cloud computing heavily relies on **encryption techniques** to secure sensitive data, but traditional cryptographic methods face potential threats from **quantum decryption capabilities**. Quantum computers, with their immense processing power, could potentially break **RSA and ECC encryption**, which currently safeguard cloud-based transactions and communications.

To counteract this, **post-quantum cryptography (PQC)** is being developed to create **quantum-resistant encryption algorithms**. Quantum encryption techniques, such as **Quantum Key Distribution (QKD)**, leverage the principles of quantum mechanics to provide **unbreakable security** for cloud-based AI applications. Cloud providers are actively exploring quantum-safe encryption methods to ensure **data integrity and privacy** in a post-quantum world.

3. Optimized Cloud Resource Management

Cloud environments depend on **efficient workload distribution, resource allocation, and dynamic scaling** to meet user demands. Quantum computing introduces **enhanced optimization techniques** that enable more intelligent **cloud resource scheduling, traffic management, and infrastructure automation**.

Quantum algorithms, such as **Shor's Algorithm** and **Grover's Algorithm**, can efficiently analyze massive datasets, leading to better **predictive analytics for cloud performance tuning**. By integrating quantum computing with **AI-driven cloud orchestration,** providers can optimize **server workloads, reduce latency, and improve overall system efficiency.**

For example, in multi-cloud environments, **quantum computing can determine the most efficient way to distribute computing workloads** across different data centers, minimizing energy consumption and cost. This breakthrough will be particularly valuable for **hyper-scale cloud providers** such as AWS, Google Cloud, and Microsoft Azure.

4. Advanced AI Algorithms and Problem Solving

Quantum-enhanced AI models can solve **complex optimization and simulation problems** that are beyond the reach of classical computing. Industries such as **drug discovery, financial modeling, and climate simulations** require **high-dimensional computations** that traditional AI struggles with. Quantum computing enhances AI's ability to **model intricate real-world systems,** leading to more **accurate predictions and data-driven insights.**

For instance, quantum-powered AI can:

- Simulate **molecular interactions** for faster drug discovery.
- Optimize **supply chain logistics** by computing multiple variables simultaneously.
- Enhance **fraud detection models** by analyzing intricate financial transactions in real-time.

By integrating quantum computing into **cloud-based AI services,** businesses can unlock **unparalleled problem-solving capabilities,** paving the way for breakthroughs in **scientific research, business analytics, and artificial intelligence.**

Challenges and Future Prospects

While quantum computing holds immense potential, several **challenges** must be addressed before it can be fully integrated with AI and cloud computing.

1. Hardware Limitations

Quantum computing is still in its **early stages** and requires highly specialized **hardware, stable quantum processors, and error correction mechanisms**. Unlike classical servers, which operate at room temperature, quantum computers need **extremely low temperatures (near absolute zero) to function effectively**. The fragility of quantum states (known as **quantum decoherence**) makes it difficult to maintain **stable and error-free computations**.

However, tech giants such as IBM, Google, and Microsoft are investing heavily in **quantum research**, developing **quantum processors and superconducting qubits** to enhance stability and scalability. As hardware advancements continue, quantum computing will become **more accessible for cloud-based AI applications**.

2. Integration with Cloud Infrastructure

Cloud providers are actively exploring **Quantum-as-a-Service (QaaS)** to integrate quantum computing capabilities into cloud platforms. Leading cloud vendors such as **AWS Braket, Google Quantum AI, and Microsoft Azure Quantum** are already offering **quantum computing environments for research and development**.

However, widespread adoption requires **seamless integration with existing cloud architectures**, enabling businesses to transition from **classical to quantum computing without disrupting operations**. Hybrid quantum-classical computing models are being developed to

bridge the gap and allow cloud users to leverage **quantum-enhanced AI algorithms** without overhauling their infrastructure.

3. Security Risks and Post-Quantum Cryptography

With the rise of quantum computing, **traditional encryption methods** used in cloud computing will become obsolete, posing a major cybersecurity risk. Organizations must adopt **post-quantum cryptographic techniques** to protect **sensitive data and cloud environments**. Governments and cybersecurity agencies are working to standardize **quantum-resistant encryption protocols**, ensuring that cloud systems remain **secure against quantum attacks**.

AI and Cloud Computing: Predictions for the Next Decade

1. AI-First Cloud Strategies

In the coming decade, organizations will increasingly shift toward **AI-driven cloud strategies** to enhance automation, operational efficiency, and security. AI will become a central force in **cloud decision-making**, helping enterprises manage workloads more effectively, reduce costs, and improve system governance. Cloud providers will integrate AI at every level, from infrastructure management to customer support, ensuring seamless cloud operations. As AI continues to evolve, businesses will depend more on intelligent automation for **predictive scaling, anomaly detection, and performance optimization**, leading to smarter cloud ecosystems.

2. Expansion of Edge AI and Cloud Synergy

The fusion of **edge computing and AI** will see rapid expansion, allowing real-time data processing closer to the source while still leveraging the cloud for **advanced analytics and long-term storage**. This shift is crucial for applications requiring **low latency**, such as autonomous vehicles, smart cities, and industrial IoT. AI-powered edge devices will handle immediate decision-making, minimizing data transmission costs and reducing cloud dependency for time-sensitive operations. Cloud providers will refine hybrid AI architectures that balance **edge processing with centralized cloud intelligence**, ensuring optimal performance and security.

3. AI-Enhanced Cloud Security and Compliance

Security remains a top concern for cloud computing, and AI will play a vital role in **fortifying cloud security** against evolving threats. AI-driven security solutions will revolutionize cloud protection by:

- **Detecting and mitigating cyber threats in real-time** through behavioral analysis and anomaly detection.
- **Automating compliance checks and regulatory reporting**, reducing human effort in maintaining industry standards.
- **Enhancing identity and access management (IAM)** by using AI-driven authentication mechanisms such as biometric security and adaptive access controls.

AI-powered security tools will proactively counter cyber risks, ensuring that cloud environments remain resilient against sophisticated attacks. Additionally, AI-driven automation will streamline regulatory adherence, helping organizations navigate complex **data privacy laws and cybersecurity compliance**.

4. Rise of AI-Powered Multi-Cloud and Hybrid Cloud Solutions

The next decade will witness a surge in **multi-cloud and hybrid cloud** adoption, as organizations aim to optimize cloud performance, cost efficiency, and security across multiple providers. AI will be instrumental in managing **complex cloud environments**, enabling businesses to:

- **Automate workload distribution** across different cloud platforms to prevent vendor lock-in.
- **Optimize cost-efficiency** by dynamically adjusting cloud resources based on real-time demand.
- **Strengthen security** through AI-driven monitoring that provides end-to-end visibility across multiple cloud environments.

AI will enable **seamless orchestration between private and public clouds**, ensuring businesses can maintain **flexibility, resilience, and operational agility**. As cloud landscapes grow more intricate, AI-driven insights will empower organizations to make data-driven decisions, leading to more **scalable and adaptive cloud architectures**.

5. Autonomous Cloud Operations and AI Governance

AI will **redefine cloud operations** by enabling **fully autonomous cloud management**, reducing the need for manual intervention. AI-driven automation will handle **infrastructure provisioning, incident resolution, and performance tuning**, ensuring cloud environments remain highly available and efficient.

Furthermore, as AI adoption in cloud computing expands, governance frameworks will become **essential** to ensure **ethical AI deployment**. Organizations will develop **AI governance policies** focusing on transparency, accountability, and bias mitigation. Regulatory bodies will also introduce stricter guidelines for **AI-driven cloud applications**, ensuring fair usage and ethical AI decision-making.

With AI-powered cloud ecosystems, businesses will experience **greater reliability, enhanced security, and improved efficiency**, shaping the future of **next-generation cloud computing**.

Summary

The future of AI in cloud computing will be characterized by increased automation, enhanced security, and revolutionary advancements such as quantum computing and self-healing infrastructure. AI-powered autonomous cloud platforms will drive efficiency, while AI-driven cybersecurity solutions will mitigate emerging threats. As AI and cloud computing continue to evolve, organizations must stay ahead by adopting innovative AI-driven cloud strategies to remain competitive in the digital landscape.

Appendices

Appendix A: Glossary of AI and Cloud Computing Terms

This glossary provides definitions of key **Artificial Intelligence (AI) and Cloud Computing** terms to help readers understand fundamental concepts and technical jargon.

1. Artificial Intelligence (AI) Terms

A

- **Algorithm**: A set of rules or steps followed by AI models to solve problems and make decisions.
- **Artificial General Intelligence (AGI)**: Hypothetical AI capable of understanding and performing any intellectual task a human can.
- **Artificial Narrow Intelligence (ANI)**: AI specialized in a specific task (e.g., speech recognition, image classification).
- **Artificial Superintelligence (ASI)**: A theoretical AI surpassing human intelligence in all aspects.

B

- **Bias in AI**: Systematic errors in AI models that lead to unfair or discriminatory outcomes.
- **Big Data**: Large datasets used for AI training, analytics, and decision-making.
- **Bayesian Network**: A probabilistic graphical model used for reasoning under uncertainty in AI.

C

- **Chatbot**: An AI-powered program that interacts with users through text or voice.
- **Cognitive Computing**: AI that mimics human thought processes, including reasoning and decision-making.
- **Computer Vision**: AI technology enables machines to analyze and interpret visual data.
- **Convolutional Neural Network (CNN)**: A deep learning model designed for image recognition tasks.
- **Clustering**: A type of unsupervised learning that groups data points with similar characteristics.

D

- **Data Augmentation**: A technique used to artificially increase the size of a dataset by applying transformations like rotation, flipping, or scaling.
- **Deep Learning (DL)**: A subset of ML using deep neural networks for complex pattern recognition.
- **Decision Tree**: A tree-like model used for classification and regression in AI.
- **Dimensionality Reduction**: A process of reducing the number of variables in a dataset to improve model efficiency.

E

- **Edge AI**: AI models running on edge devices, such as smartphones or IoT devices, instead of cloud servers.
- **Ethical AI**: AI developed with principles that ensure fairness, transparency, and accountability.
- **Explainable AI (XAI)**: AI models designed to provide transparent and interpretable decision-making processes.
- **Evolutionary Algorithms**: Optimization techniques inspired by natural selection, used in AI problem-solving.

F

- **Federated Learning**: A decentralized ML approach where models are trained across multiple devices while keeping data local.
- **Feature Engineering**: The process of selecting and transforming variables to improve ML model performance.
- **Fuzzy Logic**: A computing approach that allows for reasoning with uncertain or imprecise information.

G

- **Generative AI**: AI models that generate new data, such as text, images, or music (e.g., ChatGPT, DALL·E).
- **Gradient Descent**: An optimization algorithm used to minimize errors in ML models.
- **Graph Neural Networks (GNN)**: AI models designed to process graph-structured data.

H

- **Hyperparameter Tuning**: The process of optimizing model parameters to improve ML performance.
- **Heuristic**: A rule-of-thumb approach to problem-solving used in AI algorithms.
- **Hierarchical Clustering**: A clustering technique that builds a hierarchy of clusters based on similarity.

I

- **Inference**: The process of making predictions using a trained AI model.
- **Intelligent Agent**: An AI system capable of perceiving its environment and taking actions to achieve a goal.

- **Instance-Based Learning**: A learning approach where decisions are made based on stored examples rather than generalization.

J

- **Joint Probability Distribution**: A statistical method used in AI to model the relationship between multiple variables.

K

- **K-Means Clustering**: A popular unsupervised learning algorithm used to group data points into clusters.
- **Kernel Trick**: A technique in SVMs to transform data into a higher-dimensional space for better classification.

L

- **Latent Space**: A compressed representation of input data used in generative models.
- **Long Short-Term Memory (LSTM)**: A type of recurrent neural network (RNN) designed to handle long-term dependencies in sequential data.
- **Label Propagation**: A semi-supervised learning technique used for classification tasks.

M

- **Machine Learning (ML)**: A subset of AI where algorithms learn from data to make predictions.
- **Model Drift**: A phenomenon where an AI model's performance degrades over time due to changes in data patterns.
- **Multi-Modal AI**: AI systems that process and understand multiple types of data (e.g., text, image, speech).

- **Markov Decision Process (MDP)**: A mathematical framework used in reinforcement learning to model decision-making.

N

- **Neural Networks**: Computing systems inspired by the human brain, used in deep learning models.
- **Natural Language Processing (NLP)**: AI technology that enables computers to understand and process human language.
- **N-gram**: A sequence of 'n' words used in NLP to analyze text patterns.
- **Naïve Bayes Classifier**: A probabilistic ML model based on Bayes' Theorem used for classification tasks.

O

- **Overfitting**: A situation where an ML model learns the training data too well, leading to poor generalization on new data.
- **Optical Character Recognition (OCR)**: AI technology used to convert images of text into machine-readable text.

P

- **Predictive Analytics**: AI techniques used to predict future outcomes based on historical data.
- **Perceptron**: A basic building block of neural networks used in early AI models.
- **Principal Component Analysis (PCA)**: A dimensionality reduction technique used to improve model efficiency.

Q

- **Q-Learning**: A reinforcement learning algorithm that learns optimal actions through trial and error.

- **Quantum AI**: The integration of AI techniques with quantum computing for enhanced problem-solving.

R

- **Recurrent Neural Network (RNN)**: A neural network model used for sequential data, such as time series or speech recognition.
- **Reinforcement Learning (RL)**: A machine learning approach where an agent learns by interacting with an environment and receiving rewards or penalties.
- **Residual Networks (ResNet)**: Deep learning models designed to overcome vanishing gradient problems in training.

S

- **Supervised Learning**: A type of ML where the model learns from labeled data.
- **Semi-Supervised Learning**: A mix of labeled and unlabeled data to train an AI model.
- **Support Vector Machine (SVM)**: A supervised learning model used for classification and regression tasks.
- **Self-Supervised Learning**: A machine learning paradigm where models generate their own labels from input data.

T

- **Transformer Model**: An advanced deep learning architecture used in NLP, such as GPT and BERT.
- **Turing Test**: A test to determine if an AI can exhibit human-like intelligence in conversation.
- **Transfer Learning**: A technique where a pre-trained model is fine-tuned for a new task.

U

- **Unsupervised Learning**: A type of ML where the model finds patterns in data without labeled examples.
- **Underfitting**: A situation where an ML model is too simple and fails to capture underlying patterns in the data.

V

- **Variational Autoencoder (VAE)**: A generative AI model used to learn and generate new data distributions.
- **Vector Embeddings**: Numeric representations of data (e.g., words, images) used in AI models.

W

- **Word Embeddings**: A representation of words in vector space, used in NLP models.
- **Weak AI**: Another term for Artificial Narrow Intelligence (ANI), which specializes in specific tasks.

X

- **XGBoost**: A high-performance gradient boosting algorithm widely used in ML competitions.

Y

- **YOLO (You Only Look Once)**: A real-time object detection algorithm used in computer vision.

Z

- **Zero-Shot Learning**: A technique where an AI model recognizes patterns it has never seen before without additional training.

2. Cloud Computing Terms

A

- **API Gateway:** A managed service that allows developers to create, publish, and manage APIs.
- **Autoscaling:** The automatic adjustment of computing resources based on demand.
- **Artificial Intelligence as a Service (AIaaS):** Cloud-based AI services that provide machine learning models and tools.

B

- **Backup as a Service (BaaS):** A cloud-based solution that automates data backup and recovery.
- **Bare Metal Cloud:** A cloud service offering dedicated physical servers without virtualization.
- **Big Data:** Large-scale data processing that requires specialized cloud solutions.
- **Blockchain as a Service (BaaS):** A cloud-based solution enabling businesses to develop and manage blockchain applications.
- **Burstable Instance:** A cloud computing instance that provides baseline performance but can increase resources during demand spikes.

C

- **Cloud Computing:** The delivery of computing services (storage, processing, networking) over the internet.

- **Cloud Native:** Applications specifically built to run on cloud environments.
- **Containerization:** The use of lightweight, portable software packages (e.g., Docker) to deploy applications.
- **Content Delivery Network (CDN):** A distributed system of servers that delivers web content efficiently.

D

- **Disaster Recovery as a Service (DRaaS):** A cloud-based backup and recovery solution.
- **Data Lake:** A centralized repository storing structured and unstructured data.
- **Data Center:** A physical facility housing cloud computing infrastructure.
- **DevOps:** A set of practices that combine software development and IT operations in the cloud.

E

- **Elasticity:** The ability of a cloud system to automatically scale resources up or down based on demand.
- **Edge Computing:** Processing data closer to the source (e.g., IoT devices) rather than relying on centralized cloud servers.
- **Encryption:** The process of encoding data to protect it from unauthorized access.
- **Event-Driven Architecture:** A cloud computing model that responds to events in real-time.

F

- **Function as a Service (FaaS):** A serverless cloud computing model where applications run in response to events.
- **Federated Cloud:** A network of cloud environments that collaborate while maintaining individual autonomy.

- **Firewall as a Service (FWaaS):** Cloud-based firewall solutions that protect networks and applications.

G

- **GPU as a Service (GPUaaS):** Cloud-based access to graphical processing units for AI, ML, and high-performance computing.
- **Green Cloud Computing:** Energy-efficient cloud solutions aimed at reducing carbon footprints.

H

- **Hybrid Cloud:** A computing environment that combines on-premises infrastructure with public or private cloud services.
- **High Availability (HA):** Cloud architectures designed to minimize downtime and ensure continuous service.
- **Horizontal Scaling:** The ability to add more instances of resources to accommodate workload increases.

I

- **Infrastructure as a Service (IaaS):** A cloud computing model providing virtualized computing resources.
- **Identity and Access Management (IAM):** A security framework that ensures the right users have access to the right resources.
- **Internet of Things (IoT):** Cloud-connected devices that collect and exchange data.
- **Immutable Infrastructure:** Cloud infrastructure where components are replaced rather than modified to enhance security and stability.

J

- **Just-in-Time Provisioning:** A cloud computing model that provides resources dynamically as needed.
- **Job Scheduling:** Cloud-based workload automation and task scheduling.

K

- **Kubernetes:** An open-source container orchestration platform for managing containerized applications.
- **Key Management Service (KMS):** A cloud service for managing cryptographic keys securely.

L

- **Load Balancer:** A service that distributes incoming network traffic across multiple servers.
- **Latency:** The time delay in cloud service response and data transmission.
- **Log Management:** Cloud-based monitoring and analysis of system logs for security and performance tracking.

M

- **Multi-Cloud:** The use of multiple cloud providers to optimize performance, security, or compliance.
- **Microservices:** A cloud-native architectural approach where applications are developed as independent, loosely coupled services.
- **Machine Learning as a Service (MLaaS):** Cloud-based platforms providing machine learning tools.
- **Managed Services:** Outsourced cloud management services for infrastructure, security, and operations.

N

- **Network as a Service (NaaS):** Cloud-based networking solutions offering scalable connectivity.
- **NoSQL Database:** A cloud-native database model that supports flexible, schema-free data storage.
- **Namespace:** A logical grouping of cloud resources, often used in Kubernetes environments.

O

- **Object Storage:** A scalable cloud-based data storage model used for unstructured data.
- **Orchestration:** The automated coordination and management of cloud services and workloads.
- **Observability:** The ability to monitor cloud applications, infrastructure, and services in real-time.

P

- **Platform as a Service (PaaS):** A cloud model offering a development and deployment environment for applications.
- **Private Cloud:** A cloud environment used exclusively by a single organization.
- **Public Cloud:** A cloud environment where resources are shared among multiple users and organizations.
- **Provisioning:** The process of allocating cloud resources based on user needs.

Q

- **Quantum Computing as a Service (QCaaS):** Cloud-based quantum computing capabilities for advanced data processing.
- **Query Optimization:** AI-driven techniques to improve database performance in cloud environments.

R

- **Role-Based Access Control (RBAC):** A security framework managing cloud access based on user roles.
- **Replication:** The duplication of cloud data across multiple locations for redundancy and disaster recovery.
- **Reserved Instances:** A cloud pricing model where users commit to a specific resource usage for cost savings.

S

- **Software as a Service (SaaS):** A cloud model where applications are hosted and accessed via the internet.
- **Serverless Computing:** A cloud execution model where the cloud provider dynamically manages resource allocation.
- **Service-Level Agreement (SLA):** A contract defining service expectations between cloud providers and customers.
- **Security as a Service (SECaaS):** Cloud-based security solutions, such as firewall and threat detection.
- **Storage as a Service (STaaS):** Cloud-based data storage solutions offering scalability and flexibility.

T

- **Terraform:** An Infrastructure-as-Code (IaC) tool for cloud automation and provisioning.
- **Tenant Isolation:** Security measures that prevent data from different users from interacting in multi-tenant cloud environments.
- **Tokenization:** A cloud security measure replacing sensitive data with unique tokens for protection.

U

- **Usage-Based Billing:** A cloud pricing model where customers pay for services based on consumption.
- **Unified Threat Management (UTM):** Cloud-based security solutions integrating multiple threat detection capabilities.

V

- **Virtual Machine (VM):** A software-based simulation of a physical computer.
- **Virtual Private Cloud (VPC):** A private cloud hosted within a public cloud environment.
- **Vendor Lock-In:** A challenge where organizations become dependent on a single cloud provider's services.

W

- **Workload Management:** Cloud-based resource allocation for optimizing performance and cost.
- **Web Application Firewall (WAF):** A security solution that protects cloud applications from threats.
- **Workflow Automation:** AI-driven automation of business processes in cloud environments.

X

- **XaaS (Everything as a Service):** An umbrella term for cloud-delivered IT services, including IaaS, PaaS, and SaaS.

Y

- **YAML (Yet Another Markup Language):** A human-readable data format commonly used in cloud infrastructure automation tools.

Z

- **Zero Trust Security:** A cloud security model requiring strict identity verification for all users and devices.
- **Zone Redundancy:** Distributing cloud resources across multiple availability zones for high availability.

Appendix B: Leading AI and Cloud Computing Tools & Platforms

1. Leading AI Platforms & Tools

A. Machine Learning & AI Development Platforms

- **Google AI Platform (Vertex AI)** – A cloud-based machine learning platform offering AutoML, AI model training, and deployment services.

- **Amazon SageMaker** – A fully managed service that enables developers to build, train, and deploy ML models at scale.

- **Microsoft Azure Machine Learning** – Provides an end-to-end ML lifecycle platform for model building, training, and deployment.

- **IBM Watson AI** – AI-powered analytics and cognitive computing platform for businesses.

- **H2O.ai** – An open-source ML platform that offers AutoML and deep learning capabilities.

- **DataRobot** – An AI-driven automated machine learning (AutoML) platform for enterprises.

B. Deep Learning Frameworks

- **TensorFlow** – An open-source deep learning framework developed by Google for building neural networks.

- **PyTorch** – A flexible deep learning framework from Facebook AI Research, known for dynamic computation graphs.

- **Keras** – A high-level neural network API that runs on top of TensorFlow.

- **MXNet** – A scalable deep learning framework optimized for distributed computing.

- **Caffe** – A deep learning framework designed for speed and modularity, commonly used in image processing.

C. Natural Language Processing (NLP) Tools

- **Google Cloud Natural Language API** – NLP service that enables sentiment analysis, entity recognition, and syntax analysis.

- **OpenAI GPT (ChatGPT, GPT-4, etc.)** – A leading AI model for natural language understanding and generation.

- **spaCy** – An open-source NLP library optimized for speed and efficiency.

- **NLTK (Natural Language Toolkit)** – A library for building NLP applications in Python.

- **BERT (Bidirectional Encoder Representations from Transformers)** – Google's transformer-based NLP model for contextual understanding.

D. Computer Vision Tools

- **OpenCV** – An open-source computer vision library for image and video processing.

- **Google Cloud Vision API** – A cloud-based image analysis tool with OCR and object detection capabilities.

- **Amazon Rekognition** – A deep learning-based image and video analysis service.

- **Microsoft Azure Computer Vision** – AI-powered image processing, OCR, and object recognition service.

- **YOLO (You Only Look Once)** – A real-time object detection framework used in AI vision tasks.

2. Leading Cloud Computing Platforms & Services

A. Major Cloud Service Providers (CSPs)

- **Amazon Web Services (AWS)** – The most widely used cloud platform, offering IaaS, PaaS, and SaaS solutions.

- **Microsoft Azure** – A cloud computing platform providing AI, ML, storage, and enterprise services.

- **Google Cloud Platform (GCP)** – A cloud service suite offering AI, big data, and scalable computing solutions.

- **IBM Cloud** – AI-driven cloud computing solutions for enterprises and hybrid cloud adoption.

- **Oracle Cloud** – A cloud service offering AI, database management, and enterprise cloud solutions.

B. Cloud AI Services

- **AWS AI & ML Services (SageMaker, Rekognition, Polly, Lex, etc.)** – AI-driven cloud solutions for ML model deployment and image/audio analysis.

- **Google Cloud AI (Vertex AI, AutoML, Dialogflow, etc.)** – AI services for model training, NLP, and chatbot development.

- **Azure AI (Cognitive Services, Bot Service, AI Studio, etc.)** – AI tools for vision, speech, language, and automation.

C. Cloud Storage & Data Processing

- **Amazon S3 (Simple Storage Service)** – Scalable object storage service for data archiving and backup.

- **Google Cloud Storage** – A robust and cost-effective cloud storage solution.

- **Microsoft Azure Blob Storage** – A secure storage solution optimized for unstructured data.

- **Snowflake** – A cloud data platform specializing in data warehousing and analytics.

- **Apache Hadoop** – An open-source framework for distributed data processing.

D. Serverless Computing Services

- **AWS Lambda** – A serverless computing service that runs code in response to events.

- **Google Cloud Functions** – A serverless execution environment for deploying applications.

- **Azure Functions** – A cloud-based, event-driven serverless computing platform.

E. Containerization & Kubernetes Platforms

- **Docker** – A containerization platform that enables developers to package applications with dependencies.

- **Kubernetes (K8s)** – An open-source container orchestration system for automating deployment and scaling.

- **Amazon EKS (Elastic Kubernetes Service)** – A managed Kubernetes service on AWS.

- **Azure Kubernetes Service (AKS)** – Microsoft's managed Kubernetes service.

- **Google Kubernetes Engine (GKE)** – A cloud-based Kubernetes service for managing containerized workloads.

3. AI & Cloud Security Tools

- **AWS Shield** – A managed DDoS protection service for AWS applications.

- **Google Chronicle** – A cloud security analytics platform for threat detection.

- **Azure Sentinel** – A cloud-native SIEM tool for detecting and responding to security threats.

- **IBM QRadar** – A security intelligence and analytics tool for threat detection.

- **CrowdStrike Falcon** – A cloud-based endpoint protection platform using AI-driven threat intelligence.

4. AI & Cloud Development Tools

- **Jupyter Notebook** – An open-source web application for AI and ML research.

- **Google Colab** – A free cloud-based Jupyter notebook service with built-in GPU support.

- **PyCharm** – An integrated development environment (IDE) for Python and AI model development.

- **VS Code (Visual Studio Code)** – A lightweight and extensible IDE widely used for AI and cloud applications.

Appendix C: Recommended Research Papers & Books

1. Recommended Research Papers

A. Foundational AI Research Papers

1. **"A Few Useful Things to Know About Machine Learning"** – Pedro Domingos (2012)

    o   Explores the key principles of machine learning, model selection, and trade-offs.

    o   Source: *Communications of the ACM*

2. **"ImageNet Classification with Deep Convolutional Neural Networks"** – Alex Krizhevsky, Ilya Sutskever, Geoffrey Hinton (2012)

    o   Introduced the AlexNet architecture, which revolutionized deep learning and image processing.

    o   Source: *Advances in Neural Information Processing Systems (NeurIPS)*

3. **"Attention Is All You Need"** – Ashish Vaswani et al. (2017)

    o   Introduced the Transformer model, which powers modern NLP models like GPT and BERT.

    o   Source: *Advances in Neural Information Processing Systems (NeurIPS)*

4. **"Generative Adversarial Nets (GANs)"** – Ian Goodfellow et al. (2014)

    o   Introduced GANs, a breakthrough in generative AI for image and data synthesis.

    o   Source: *NeurIPS*

5. **"Deep Residual Learning for Image Recognition"** – Kaiming He et al. (2015)

- Proposed ResNet, which significantly improved deep learning models by solving vanishing gradient problems.

- Source: *CVPR*

B. Research Papers on AI in Cloud Computing

6. **"Cloud Computing and Emerging IT Platforms: Vision, Hype, and Reality for Delivering Computing as the 5th Utility"** – Rajkumar Buyya et al. (2009)

   - Defines cloud computing, its architectural principles, and challenges.

   - Source: *Future Generation Computer Systems*

7. **"A Survey of Machine Learning for Big Data Processing"** – Taleb Larbi, Nabil El Ioini (2020)

   - Reviews ML techniques used in large-scale cloud computing environments.

   - Source: *IEEE Transactions on Big Data*

8. **"Serverless Computing: Current Trends and Open Problems"** – Eric Jonas et al. (2019)

   - Examines serverless computing, its benefits, and challenges in cloud architectures.

   - Source: *arXiv*

9. **"Artificial Intelligence and Cloud Computing: Benefits, Risks, and Ethical Considerations"** – Kate Crawford, Timnit Gebru (2021)

   - Discusses AI ethics, cloud security risks, and AI biases in cloud applications.

   - Source: *ACM Digital Library*

10. **"Fog and Edge Computing: Enhancing Cloud AI for Low-Latency Applications"** – Flavio Bonomi, Rodolfo Milito (2018)

- Explores edge computing for AI-driven cloud applications and its role in IoT.

- Source: *IEEE Communications Magazine*

C. Research Papers on AI and Cloud Security

11. **"Privacy-Preserving Machine Learning in Cloud Environments"** – Nicholas Papernot et al. (2017)

- Discusses techniques like differential privacy and federated learning in AI cloud security.

- Source: *IEEE Transactions on Information Forensics and Security*

12. **"Cloud Security and AI: A Comprehensive Survey"** – Tariq M. Alassafi et al. (2022)

- Covers AI-based security solutions in cloud environments, including intrusion detection systems.

- Source: *ACM Computing Surveys*

13. **"Adversarial Machine Learning in the Cloud"** – Ian Goodfellow et al. (2020)

- Explores adversarial attacks and their impact on AI models hosted in cloud environments.

- Source: *IEEE Security & Privacy*

2. Recommended Books

A. Books on Artificial Intelligence

1. **"Artificial Intelligence: A Modern Approach"** – Stuart Russell, Peter Norvig (4th Edition, 2020)

   o The most widely used textbook on AI, covering everything from search algorithms to deep learning.

2. **"Deep Learning"** – Ian Goodfellow, Yoshua Bengio, Aaron Courville (2016)

o An in-depth guide on deep learning principles, covering CNNs, RNNs, and GANs.

3. **"Hands-On Machine Learning with Scikit-Learn, Keras, and TensorFlow"** – Aurélien Géron (3rd Edition, 2022)

   o A practical approach to machine learning using Python and modern AI frameworks.

4. **"The Hundred-Page Machine Learning Book"** – Andriy Burkov (2019)

   o A concise and beginner-friendly introduction to machine learning.

5. **"Superintelligence: Paths, Dangers, Strategies"** – Nick Bostrom (2014)

   o Explores the risks and future implications of artificial intelligence.

B. Books on Cloud Computing

6. **"Cloud Computing: Principles and Paradigms"** – Rajkumar Buyya, James Broberg, Andrzej Goscinski (2011)

   o A foundational book explaining cloud computing architectures, virtualization, and service models.

7. **"Architecting the Cloud: Design Decisions for Cloud Computing Service Models"** – Michael J. Kavis (2014)

   o A practical guide to cloud architecture, covering IaaS, PaaS, and SaaS models.

8. **"Cloud Native Patterns: Designing Change-Tolerant Software"** – Cornelia Davis (2019)

   o Covers best practices for developing cloud-native applications.

9. **"Serverless Computing: Economic and Architectural Impact"** – Bastian Venthur (2021)

o   Discusses the rise of serverless computing and its impact on cloud costs and scalability.

10. **"Cloud Security Handbook: Best Practices for Securing Cloud Environments"** – Eyal Estrin (2022)

- A comprehensive guide to cloud security challenges and solutions.

C. Books on AI in Cloud Computing

11. **"Machine Learning Engineering in the Cloud"** – Carl Osipov (2021)

- Covers MLOps, AI model deployment, and cloud AI services on AWS, GCP, and Azure.

12. **"AI and Cloud Computing: From Theory to Practice"** – Xiaolin Li, Judy Qiu (2020)

- Explores the intersection of AI and cloud technologies in modern computing.

13. **"The AI-First Company: How to Compete and Win with Artificial Intelligence"** – Ash Fontana (2021)

- Discusses how businesses can leverage AI and cloud technologies for competitive advantage.

Appendix D: Case Study References and Industry Reports

This appendix provides a curated collection of case studies and industry reports showcasing real-world implementations of AI in cloud computing. These references offer insights into successful AI-driven cloud transformations, security concerns, and emerging trends across various industries.

1. Case Study References

A. AI-Powered Cloud Transformation in Enterprises

1. **Microsoft AI and Azure: Coca-Cola's Digital Transformation**

   o Coca-Cola leveraged Microsoft Azure AI for data analytics, customer insights, and intelligent automation.

   o **Key Takeaways:** Improved supply chain efficiency, AI-driven customer engagement, and predictive analytics.

   o **Source:** Microsoft Case Study Portal

2. **Google Cloud AI: Target's Personalized Shopping Experience**

   o Target implemented AI-powered cloud analytics on Google Cloud to enhance personalized marketing.

   o **Key Takeaways:** Increased customer retention, AI-driven recommendations, and efficient data processing.

   o **Source:** Google Cloud Case Studies

3. **AWS AI & Machine Learning: Netflix's AI-Driven Content Recommendations**

   o Netflix uses AWS cloud-based AI models for content personalization and recommendation engines.

- o **Key Takeaways:** Optimized user experience, enhanced content delivery, and scalable cloud AI infrastructure.

- o **Source:** AWS Case Study Library

4. **IBM Watson and AI in Healthcare: Mayo Clinic's Precision Medicine**

- o Mayo Clinic integrated IBM Watson AI with cloud services to enhance diagnosis and patient treatment.

- o **Key Takeaways:** AI-driven diagnostics, improved patient outcomes, and scalable cloud computing.

- o **Source:** IBM Research & Watson Case Studies

5. **Oracle Cloud AI: AI-Powered Predictive Maintenance for GE Aviation**

- o GE Aviation utilized Oracle Cloud AI for real-time aircraft engine monitoring and predictive maintenance.

- o **Key Takeaways:** Reduced maintenance costs, minimized downtime, and optimized operational efficiency.

- o **Source:** Oracle Cloud Customer Stories

B. AI and Cloud Security Case Studies

6. **AI-Driven Cloud Security: Palo Alto Networks' Prisma Cloud in Financial Services**

- o Prisma Cloud's AI-driven security monitoring and threat detection improved cybersecurity for financial institutions.

- o **Key Takeaways:** AI-powered anomaly detection, cloud security automation, and regulatory compliance.

- o **Source:** Palo Alto Networks Case Studies

7. **Microsoft Defender AI and Cloud Security: HSBC's Fraud Detection System**

   o HSBC deployed AI-powered fraud detection using Microsoft Defender and Azure cloud security tools.

   o **Key Takeaways:** Real-time fraud prevention, AI-driven transaction monitoring, and improved compliance.

   o **Source:** Microsoft Security Blog

8. **AWS GuardDuty AI in Cloud Security: Capital One's Data Protection Strategy**

   o Capital One enhanced cloud security using AWS GuardDuty and AI-driven risk assessments.

   o **Key Takeaways:** Automated threat intelligence, enhanced data protection, and AI-powered cloud monitoring.

   o **Source:** AWS Security Case Studies

9. **Google Cloud AI in Cybersecurity: Chronicle and AI Threat Detection**

   o Google's Chronicle AI platform improved threat intelligence and cloud security for enterprises.

   o **Key Takeaways:** AI-driven malware detection, behavioral analytics, and proactive security measures.

   o **Source:** Google Cloud Security Reports

10. **IBM Cloud Security and AI: AI-Driven Incident Response at IBM X-Force**

   • IBM X-Force used AI-driven cloud security analytics for incident response and threat management.

   • **Key Takeaways:** AI-enhanced threat hunting, automated security operations, and cloud SIEM integration.

   • **Source:** IBM Cloud Security Reports

2. Industry Reports on AI in Cloud Computing

A. AI and Cloud Computing Market Trends

11. **Gartner Report: Top Trends in AI-Powered Cloud Computing (2024)**

- Examines AI adoption in cloud computing and emerging trends in AI-driven cloud services.

- **Key Insights:** AI-driven cloud automation, serverless computing growth, and AI security challenges.

- **Source:** Gartner Research

12. **McKinsey & Company: The AI and Cloud Revolution in Enterprise IT (2023)**

- Explores AI's role in cloud transformation and enterprise cloud strategies.

- **Key Insights:** AI-driven cost optimization, AI for cloud automation, and multi-cloud AI architectures.

- **Source:** McKinsey Technology Reports

13. **Forrester Research: AI in Cloud Computing – State of the Industry Report (2024)**

- Analysis of AI adoption in cloud platforms and enterprise cloud AI deployments.

- **Key Insights:** AI-driven DevOps, AI security automation, and cloud-based AI model deployment.

- **Source:** Forrester Cloud Reports

14. **IDC Research: AI and Cloud Computing – Growth & Investment Trends (2023-2030)**

- Market forecast on AI-driven cloud investments and future cloud AI applications.

- **Key Insights:** AI for cloud infrastructure, AI governance in cloud environments, and AI ethics in cloud computing.

- **Source:** IDC Research Reports

15. **Accenture Technology Vision: AI & Cloud Computing – The Next Decade (2024)**

- Predicts the future impact of AI on cloud computing and industry innovations.

- **Key Insights:** AI-driven cloud sustainability, AI-powered cloud automation, and industry-specific AI cloud use cases.

- **Source:** Accenture Cloud Innovation Reports

B. Cloud Security and AI Industry Reports

16. **Cybersecurity and Infrastructure Security Agency (CISA) Report: AI-Driven Cloud Security (2023)**

- Discusses AI's role in strengthening cloud security and mitigating cyber threats.

- **Key Insights:** AI-powered threat detection, cloud security best practices, and regulatory compliance.

- **Source:** CISA Cybersecurity Reports

17. **MIT Technology Review: AI for Cloud Security – Innovations and Risks (2023)**

- Analyzes AI's impact on cloud security, AI-driven SIEM, and cloud attack detection.

- **Key Insights:** AI-powered security automation, AI for zero-trust cloud architectures, and machine learning in cloud SOCs.

- **Source:** MIT Technology Review Reports

18. **Cloud Security Alliance (CSA): AI in Cloud Security – Emerging Standards (2024)**

- Defines AI security frameworks and best practices for cloud computing environments.

- **Key Insights:** AI compliance, AI-driven incident response, and AI governance in cloud security.

- **Source:** Cloud Security Alliance Reports

19. **IBM Security Report: AI-Powered Threat Intelligence in the Cloud (2023)**

- Discusses AI-driven threat intelligence solutions for cloud security.

- **Key Insights:** AI-driven malware detection, AI-enhanced endpoint security, and AI-powered cloud SOCs.

- **Source:** IBM Security Intelligence Reports

20. **Deloitte Cloud AI Report: AI for Cloud Compliance and Risk Management (2023)**

- Examines how AI helps automate compliance in cloud environments.

- **Key Insights:** AI-driven risk assessments, cloud security audits, and AI for regulatory compliance.

- **Source:** Deloitte Cloud Compliance Reports

Appendix E: Python Code for AI-Driven Cloud Computing Solutions

This appendix provides **Python scripts** and **cloud automation techniques** for integrating AI-driven solutions in cloud computing. It covers:

- **Setting Up AI in Cloud Environments** (AWS, Azure, GCP)

- **Building AI Models on Cloud-Based Infrastructure**

- **AI-Powered Cloud Automation and Security Scripts**

- **AI-Driven Cloud Cost Optimization**

- **AI for Cloud Compliance & Governance**

- **AI-Powered Cloud Incident Response & Self-Healing Infrastructure**

1. Setting Up AI in a Cloud Environment

A. Deploying AI Services on AWS Using SageMaker

```python
python
import boto3

sagemaker_client = boto3.client('sagemaker')

# Create an AI-powered SageMaker instance
response = sagemaker_client.create_notebook_instance(
    NotebookInstanceName='AI-Cloud-Instance',
    InstanceType='ml.m5.large',
    RoleArn='arn:aws:iam::123456789012:role/SageMakerExecutionRole'
)
```

```
print("SageMaker AI instance created:", response)
```

B. Deploying AI Models on Azure AI Services

```python
python

from azure.ai.ml import MLClient

from azure.identity import DefaultAzureCredential


ml_client = MLClient(DefaultAzureCredential(), "<subscription_id>",
"<resource_group>")


model = ml_client.models.create_or_update(

    name="AI-Cloud-Model",

    path="model/",

    description="AI model deployed on Azure"

)


print("Model deployed successfully on Azure AI Services")
```

C. Deploying AI on Google Cloud AI Platform (Vertex AI)

```python
python

from google.cloud import aiplatform


aiplatform.init(project="your-project-id", location="us-central1")


model = aiplatform.Model.upload(

    display_name="AI-Cloud-Model",

    artifact_uri="gs://your-bucket-path/",
```

```
   serving_container_image_uri="us-docker.pkg.dev/vertex-
ai/prediction/sklearn-cpu.1-0:latest"

)
```

```
print("AI Model Deployed on Google Cloud AI")
```

2. Building AI Models on Cloud-Based Infrastructure

A. Training a Machine Learning Model on AWS SageMaker

```python
import sagemaker

from sagemaker.sklearn import SKLearn


sklearn_estimator = SKLearn(
    entry_point="train.py",
    framework_version="0.23-1",
    instance_type="ml.m5.large",
    role="arn:aws:iam::123456789012:role/SageMakerExecutionRole"
)


sklearn_estimator.fit({"train": "s3://your-bucket/train.csv"})
```

B. Deploying a TensorFlow Model on Azure ML

```python
from azure.ai.ml.entities import Model

from azure.ai.ml import MLClient


ml_client = MLClient(DefaultAzureCredential(), "<subscription_id>",
"<resource_group>")
```

```
model = Model(
    name="tensorflow-cloud-ai",
    path="outputs/model/",
    description="AI model trained on Azure ML",
)


ml_client.models.create_or_update(model)
print("Model deployed on Azure ML")
```

3. AI-Powered Cloud Automation and Security Scripts

A. AI-Based Anomaly Detection in Cloud Logs (AWS CloudWatch & AI)

```python
python
import boto3
import json
import numpy as np
from sklearn.ensemble import IsolationForest


client = boto3.client('logs')


response = client.describe_log_streams(
    logGroupName='your-log-group'
)


log_events = response['logStreams']
```

```
log_data = [json.loads(event['logStreamName']) for event in log_events]


model = IsolationForest(n_estimators=100, contamination=0.1)

anomalies = model.fit_predict(np.array(log_data))


print("Anomalies detected:", anomalies)
```

B. AI-Driven Auto-Healing Cloud Infrastructure (Google Cloud AI + Terraform)

```python
python
import google.cloud.logging
from google.cloud import monitoring_v3


client = google.cloud.logging.Client()
monitoring_client = monitoring_v3.MetricServiceClient()


project_name = "projects/your-project-id"
metric_filter =
'metric.type="compute.googleapis.com/instance/cpu/utilization"'


results = monitoring_client.list_time_series(
    request={"name": project_name, "filter": metric_filter, "interval":
{"end_time": {"seconds": 60}}},
)


for result in results:
    if result.points[0].value.double_value > 0.8:
        print("High CPU usage detected. Initiating auto-scaling...")
```

> # Auto-scale logic using Terraform or Kubernetes

4. AI-Driven Cloud Cost Optimization

A. AI-Powered AWS Cost Analysis & Optimization

```python
import boto3

client = boto3.client('ce')

response = client.get_cost_and_usage(
    TimePeriod={'Start': '2024-03-01', 'End': '2024-03-31'},
    Granularity='MONTHLY',
    Metrics=['BlendedCost']
)

print("AWS Cost Analysis:", response)
```

B. Predicting Future Cloud Costs Using AI (AWS Cost Forecasting)

```python
import numpy as np
from sklearn.linear_model import LinearRegression

# Sample past cloud costs
costs = np.array([100, 120, 150, 170, 200]).reshape(-1, 1)
months = np.array([1, 2, 3, 4, 5]).reshape(-1, 1)

model = LinearRegression()
```

```
model.fit(months, costs)


# Predict future costs

future_months = np.array([6, 7, 8]).reshape(-1, 1)

predicted_costs = model.predict(future_months)


print("Predicted Cloud Costs for Next 3 Months:", predicted_costs)
```

5. AI for Cloud Compliance & Governance

A. AI-Powered Compliance Checks on AWS (AWS Config & AI)

```python
python
import boto3


client = boto3.client('config')


response = client.describe_compliance_by_resource(
    ResourceType='AWS::S3::Bucket'
)

print("AWS Compliance Report:", response)
```

6. AI-Powered Cloud Incident Response

A. AI-Based Incident Detection & Auto-Mitigation (Google Cloud Security Command Center)

```python
python
from google.cloud import securitycenter


client = securitycenter.SecurityCenterClient()
```

```
# Fetch security findings
project_id = "your-project-id"
org_name = f"organizations/{project_id}"


findings = client.list_findings(request={"parent": org_name})


for finding in findings:
    if "threat" in finding.finding.category.lower():
        print("Security threat detected:", finding)
        # Implement auto-mitigation
```